T0063352

The Greatest Religious Question

Why Are Believers Like Kings, Popes, Presidents, Prime Ministers, Politicians, Pastors, Prophets and Bishops in the Third Heaven but Not Sure of the First Heaven/God's Kingdom?

BROTHER DONALD SWEETING

WestBow Press books may be ordered through booksellers or by contacting:

WestBow Press
A Division of Thomas Nelson & Zondervan
1663 Liberty Drive
Bloomington, IN 47403
www.westbowpress.com
1 (866) 928-1240

ISBN: 978-1-4908-5833-3 (sc)
ISBN: 978-1-4908-5834-0 (hc)
ISBN: 978-1-4908-5835-7 (e)

Library of Congress Control Number: 2014919536

Printed in the United States of America.

WestBow Press rev. date: 11/20/2014

Contents

(1) A Sermon for All Times 1
(2) Are You a Jew or a Gentile? 25
(3) The Greatest Religious Question 47
(4) Why Did Jesus (God) Come to Earth in the Flesh? 67
(5) A Mysterious Woman of the Bible 75
(6) A Closer Look at Two Saves 83
(7) Can The Rich Enter Heaven? (Hardly) 87
(8) Marriage and Divorce 93
(9) Is It Really Love When We Say, "I Love You"? 100
(10) Works of the Holy Spirit 108
(11) A Look at the Family 112
(12) What Is Your Relationship with God? 115
(13) Jesus' Twelve Disciples 118
(14) Highlight These Scriptures In Your Holy Bible 120
(15) How-to Pray 124
(16) My Favorite Testimony 128

Acknowledgments 131

(1)

A Sermon for All Times

This is your map to salvation-it lays out the itinerary Jesus gave that will take us to the Father's heaven. To fully understand this sermon, you must know the answers to three questions:

(1) Where are the three heavens?
(2) How are there two acts that save?
(3) How are the Father, Son, and Holy Ghost one?

The three heavens are all found in Genesis 1. We see in Genesis 1:1 that God created the first heaven where He dwells and then He created the earth. God took six days to create the earth, and He went back to His heaven to rest. How many days do you think He took to create His heaven? We understand that this development is still being carried out in the Father's house, as we find in John 14:2. Remember that the earth is only a footstool unto the Lord, as Jesus said in Matthew 5:34–35: "But I say unto you, Swear not at all; neither by heaven; for it is God's throne: nor by the earth; for it is his footstool: neither by Jerusalem; for it is the city of the great King." John informed us that no one has gone to the first heaven: "And no man hath ascended up to heaven, but he that came down from heaven, even the Son of man which is in heaven" (John 3:13).

Second, God made the second heaven outside this world, where He placed the sun, moon, and stars to give light to the earth: "And God made two great lights; the greater light to rule the day, and the lesser light to rule the night: he made the stars also. And God set them in the firmament of the heaven to give light upon the earth" (Genesis 1:16–17).

Now many people teach that the Father dwells in the third heaven. This, as you will see, is not the truth. God made the third heaven between the sea and the clouds where the birds fly.

> And God said, Let there be a firmament in the midst of the waters, and let it divide the waters from the waters. And God made the firmament, and divided the waters [sea] which were under the firmament from the waters [clouds] which were above the firmament: and it was so. And God called the firmament Heaven. And the evening and the morning were the second day. And God said, let the waters bring forth abundantly the moving creature [fish] that hath life, and fowl [birds] that may fly above the earth in the open firmament of heaven. (Genesis 1:6–8, 20)

Here is why this is not the heaven where God dwells. In two days, He made two heavens, whereas in Genesis 1:1 He made one heaven before He made the earth. Let us give some serious thought to this; who would want to think God the Father would be third class in anything? He is the deity and is always first, second to none. Jesus referred to this third heaven as paradise in Luke 23:43, where He took the condemned man on the cross. This is not the paradise in the Father's heaven because no one has ever gone there, and Jesus will only take the saints there when the Father gives Him the go-ahead to come back and receive the saints—His sheep—into God's paradise. There they shall eat of the tree of life and live forever, as Revelation 2:7 promises us.

The apostle Paul also referred to the third heaven and paradise as being the same place. Let us read how Paul put them together.

> I knew a man in Christ above fourteen years ago, (whether in the body, I cannot tell; or whether out of the body, I cannot tell: God knoweth;) such a one caught up to the third heaven. And I knew such a man, (whether in the body, or out of the body, I cannot tell: God knoweth;) How that he was caught up into paradise, and heard unspeakable words, which it is not lawful for a man to utter. (2 Corinthians 12:2–4)

Jesus also referred to the third heaven-paradise, in Matthew 24:31, which tells how He will send His holy angels to gather the saints when He returns from the first heaven: "And he shall send his angels with a great sound of a trumpet, and they shall gather together his elect from the four winds, from one end of heaven to the other" (Matthew 24:31).

The question about God's two acts to save finds its explanation in John 11:26, Matthew 16:28, and John 6:44. The first act to lead to one being saved is to believe that Jesus Christ is the Messiah and the Son of God. Let us read what Jesus said to Martha while on the way to the grave of Lazarus, her brother. John 11:26 states, "And whosoever liveth and believeth in me shall never die. Believest thou this?" John 3:18 says that if one does not believe, then one is condemned already. Those of us whose parents believe are born saved. We understood this from Matthew 18:6, where Jesus refers to the little children who believed in Him; they believed because their parents believed. A child accounts for his or her own sins at the age of twelve. This is the first way that one can be saved. One can lose one's salvation if one stops believing that Jesus is the Son of God. One can, however, have a change of mind at any time and again believe that Jesus is the Son of God and become saved again because one believes. See John 1:12 for an insight into this. If one does not work, according to Luke 6:46, then one will die when Jesus returns to paradise. As Matthew 16:28 reminds us, "Verily I say unto you, there be some standing here, which shall not taste of death, till they see the Son of man coming in his kingdom."

The second way to being saved, where only the Father can save you the second time, happens when He draws you to His Son, Jesus. Everyone who comes into this world should ask the Father to use him or her in the harvest or to draw him or her unto His Son. He is seeking from the heart those He will save (John 4:23). Only God converts (Luke 22:32). Peter, who cast demons out of people, was saved in the first sense but not in the second way (not converted). When the Father saves you Himself, you cannot lose this salvation, as the gospel tells us in John 10:27–29.

The third question asks, "How are the Father, Son, and Holy Ghost one?" As 1 John 5:7 said, the Father, the Word, and the Holy Ghost record what we do and these three are one. In addition, Jesus said in John 10:20 that He and the Father are one. The Holy Spirit has given me the understanding that the Father is the body, the Word is the Son, and the mouth of God and the Holy Ghost is the power and the hand of God.

Before I go into the sermon, (here is the itinerary) let me simplify it. The heavenly Father is going to destroy this earth by fire, as Revelation 8:7 and 13 reminds us. Before He does so, He is inviting all who would believe and serve Him from the heart to eat at His table. The first time God sent an invitation by Noah, the prophet, but the people did not receive it. God saved lives in the ark, a large boat, and He destroyed the earth by water (Genesis 7:23). This time He sent the invitation to His people the Jews with His Son Jesus the Christ, but they did not receive it. Then He sent the invitation to the Gentiles by a converted Jew called Saul who changed his name to Paul. The Father wants to save lives in His kingdom (the first heaven) and destroy this earth by fire. Don't worry about prophecies and what will take place after this life. First, believe that Jesus is the Son of God (John 3:16–18). Second, do well to all humankind (Matthew 5:16). And third, pray that the Father will draw you unto His Son (John 6:44), that Jesus will put you on His right hand as a sheep when He returns to receive everyone the Father has drawn unto Him (Matthew 25:31–34), and take them to the Father (Mark 8:38 – Revelation 5:1-8).

The sermon for all times calls us both to believe and to do. John the Baptist preached it; Jesus and His disciples preached it. The Jews did not receive it. Jesus sent Paul to the Gentiles to preach it. The Holy Spirit sent me with it. Why do we say we believe, but yet we do not what God asks of us? And the Father, if He has not already chosen you, wants to send you to teach it; if only to friends, family, and co-workers. Many believe, but few will do. Many are ashamed of the gospel, thank God for you.

Jesus said, "Believe that I am the Christ and you are saved." This is the first save, and there is nothing anyone can do to second save you; only the Father will give you this salvation, by converting you and drawing you unto His Son, according to what you do while you are here on earth. Let your light shine before others so they may see your good works and glorify the Father who is in heaven. Pray that the Father will draw you unto His Son, and also pray that He will send more laborers into the harvest.

The Holy Spirit led me to understand that more than 95 percent of the Bahamian people (of the Bahamas, with a small population about sixty miles from the east coast of Florida) believe and are saved in the first sense. It doesn't matter how many sins you have committed; if you believe that Jesus is the Christ and the Messiah, you are saved. The condemned man who was hanging on the cross believed, and he was saved (Luke 23:43). But with this save, one can lose one's salvation by not believing that Jesus is the Son of God. It's as if you put your hands to the plow and then look back. This means you let some other religious group persuade you that Jesus is not the Son of God. Jesus asked the Jews a question in Luke 6:46: "Why call ye me Lord, Lord and do not the things that I say?" No matter how little you have; help the needy with a good heart, looking for nothing in return. Jesus said that the least we have done for one of these, we have done it for Him.

This next passage from the Scriptures is very, very important for us to know. What Jesus said at that time applies today; all who believe that Jesus is the Son of God are saved and will not die. But if they do not carry out the commandments of Jesus before they leave this earth so that the Father may draw them unto Jesus, then they will go into paradise-heaven, and when Jesus returns, they will die. Here is the Scripture; we must understand and believe. Jesus said in Matthew 16:28, "Verily I say unto you, there be some standing here, which shall not taste of death, till they see the Son of man coming in his kingdom." If we believe that Jesus is the Son of God and do His commands, we must pray to the Father in Jesus' name and ask the Father to draw us unto His Son then we will be saved forevermore.

Let us now look at some of the Scriptures so we may have a clear view of Jesus' message; first we must understand six things in the Bible that we have likely overlooked.

(1) Jesus never came to the Gentiles.

> But he answered and said, I am not sent but unto the lost sheep of the house of Israel. (Matthew 15:24)

> These twelve Jesus sent forth, and commanded them, saying, Go not into the way of the Gentiles, and into any city of the Samaritans enter ye not: But go rather to the lost sheep of the house of Israel. (Matthew 10:5–6)

These sayings of Jesus are often overlooked by many preachers of the gospel. Some also seek their own logical reasons why we should believe that Jesus came to the Gentiles. After Jesus went back to heaven and the Father told Him to compel the Gentiles to come into His kingdom, He said the following:

> And the lord said unto the servant, Go out into the highways and hedges, and compel them to come in, that my house may be filled. (Luke 14:23). Jesus then blinded Saul-Paul.

> And he fell to the earth, and heard a voice saying unto him, Saul, Saul, why persecutest thou me? And he said, who art thou, Lord? And the Lord said I am Jesus whom thou persecutest: it is hard for thee to kick against the pricks. And he trembling and astonished said, Lord, what wilt thou have me to do? And the Lord said unto him, Arise, and go into the city, and it shall be told thee what thou must do. And the men which journeyed with him stood speechless, hearing a voice, but seeing no man. And Saul arose from the earth; and when his eyes were opened, he saw no man: but they led him by the hand, and brought him into Damascus. And he was three days without sight, and neither did eat nor drink. (Acts 9:4–9)

Jesus gave Saul his sight back that he takes the message unto the Gentiles.

> And there was a certain disciple at Damascus, named Ananias; and to him said the Lord in a vision, Ananias. And he said, Behold, I am here, Lord. And the Lord said unto him, Arise, and go into the street which is called Straight, and enquire in the house of Judas for one called Saul, of Tarsus: for, behold, he prayeth, And hath seen in a vision a man named Ananias coming in, and putting his hand on him, that he might receive his sight. Then Ananias answered, Lord, I have heard by many of this man, how much evil he hath done to thy saints at Jerusalem: And here he hath authority from the chief priests to bind all that call on thy name. But the Lord said unto him, Go thy way: for he is a chosen vessel unto me, to bear my name before the Gentiles, and kings, and the children of Israel. (Acts 9:10–15)

(2) Jesus said that we worship in vain because we follow commands of men.

> This people draweth nigh unto me with their mouth, and honoureth me with their lips; but their heart is far from me. But in vain they

> do worship me, teaching for doctrines the commandments of men. (Matthew 15:8–9)

We must realize that the greatest commandment of man is the altar call. "Come to Jesus; He will save you. Give Him your heart. Let Him come into your heart." All of these are vain, null, void, and wrong. Jesus said you cannot come to Him unless the Father draws you unto Him. Pray that the Father will draw you unto Jesus. Too many people are following that commandment, "Come to the altar." That is why Jesus said that when He returns to paradise/heaven, many will be turned away.

(3) Jesus said that He will build His church, and He was not talking about a building. We must realize that not all believers are the church. False prophets and wolves dressed in sheep clothing believe but Jesus will not use them to build His church. Many believers in the third heaven that followed the commandments of men; the Father has not drawn them to Jesus therefore Jesus was not able to use them in the building of His church, they would be turned away when Jesus return to paradise. Matthew 8:11-12.

> And I say also unto thee, that thou art Peter, and upon this rock I will build my church; and the gates of hell shall not prevail against it. (Matthew 16:18)

No building should be called the church. It causes people to confuse the body of converted believers in Christ with the building. In all seven letters Jesus sent unto the churches of Asia (Revelation chapters 1 and 2) He said, "Hear what the Spirit is saying unto the churches." The Spirit will not speak to a building. Here is what Jesus said to the disciples when they showed Him the beautiful stones of the temple:

> And Jesus said unto them, See ye not all these things? Verily I say unto you, there shall not be left here one stone upon another that shall not be thrown down. (Matthew 24:2)

At this time the temple is no more, and a mosque is built on the site where the temple was. We cannot worship the Father in a building. Jesus said it, and we must believe it. We worship not in the Holy City, not in the synagogues, and not on the street corners. Matthew 6:5 says, "And when thou prayest, thou shalt not be as the hypocrites are: for they love to pray standing in the synagogues and in the corners of the streets, that they may be seen of men. Verily I say unto you, they have their reward."

(4) Why do we call any man or any preacher of the gospel a pastor, a shepherd, our father, or anything above minister or brother? Hear what Jesus said to His disciples:

> But be not ye called Rabbi: for one is your Master, even Christ; and all ye are brethren. And call no man your father upon the earth: for one is your Father, which is in heaven. Neither be ye called masters: for one is your Master, even Christ. But he that is greatest among you shall be your servant. And whosoever shall exalt himself shall be abased; and he that shall humble himself shall be exalted. (Matthew 23:8–12)

> But Jesus called them unto him, and said, Ye know that the princes of the Gentiles exercise dominion over them, and they that are great exercise authority upon them. But it shall not be so among you: but whosoever will be great among you, let him be your minister; And whosoever will be chief among you, let him be your servant: Even as the Son of man came not to be ministered unto, but to minister, and to give his life a ransom for many. (Matthew 20:25–28)

A minister is a servant unto the brethren, not the brethren a servant unto the minister. We are not greater than Jesus' disciples, and therefore we should abide in His instructions. In John 10:11–15, Jesus said that no one can be a shepherd of His sheep, but he who is a hireling (one who is paid to do a job) cares not for the sheep. Anyone who becomes a shepherd is equal to Jesus, and anyone who takes a position above shepherd appears to be greater than the shepherd but is not; Jesus called him/her a hireling. Think about this—if I say I love my Father, who do you think I mean: my heavenly Father, my dad, or a priest? God knows the heart, yes, but Jesus said we must call no man Father upon the earth in Matthew 23:9, as we read above.

The Father does not share His name or glory with any man. We must understand that all those who have high positions and big names are not second saved; yes, they will do many wonderful works in Jesus' name and go into the third heaven/paradise, but to their disappointment, Jesus will not take them to the Father because they chose to seek a higher position than Jesus, which is of the world, and the Father will not draw them unto His Son. Let us read what Jesus said in Matthew 7:21–23.

> Not everyone that saith unto me, Lord, Lord, shall enter into the kingdom of heaven; but he that doeth the will of my Father which is in heaven. Many will say to me in that day, Lord, Lord, have we not prophesied in thy name? And in thy name have cast out devils? And in thy name done many wonderful works? And then will I profess unto them, I never knew you: depart from me, ye that work iniquity.

Let us see the seriousness of this matter. No Jew will be called a bishop or pope; these are positions of the

Gentiles (people the Father told His Son bring in from the highways). How presumptuous are we. We were only invited to the Father's house through grace and mercy because the Father's special guests (the Jews) turned down His invitation. Why then would we want to take on higher positions than God's Son and His disciples? Even though we heard Jesus instructed His disciples not to be called anything higher than brethren, yet we seek big names and fame to impress men. Here is what Jesus had to say about that in Luke 16:15: "And he said unto them, ye are they which justify yourselves before men; but God knoweth your hearts: for that which is highly esteemed among men is abomination in the sight of God."

(5) There are no true prophets or prophetesses on this earth today. Jesus said the last prophet was John the Baptist. We read in Luke 16:16, "The law and the prophets were until John: since that time the kingdom of God is preached, and every man presseth into it." (See also Matthew 11:13.) There are people the Lord speaks to by the Holy Spirit, but there is no direct contact with the Father to man, bypassing the Son of God. Here is what Jesus said in John 14:16–17 and 25–26:

> And I will pray the Father, and he shall give you another Comforter that he may abide with you forever; Even the Spirit of truth; whom the world cannot receive, because it seeth him not, neither knoweth him: but ye

> know him; for he dwelleth with you, and shall be in you … These things have I spoken unto you, being yet present with you. But the Comforter, which is the Holy Ghost, whom the Father will send in my name, he shall teach you all things, and bring all things to your remembrance, whatsoever I have said unto you.

All of those who call themselves prophets today are false prophets. We understand that prophets brought laws directly from the Father to man. If there are no more prophets, then there is no more law to come. Matthew 7:15 says, "Beware of false prophets, which come to you in sheep's clothing, but inwardly they are ravening wolves."

(6) The question is often asked, what is the right amount should I pay for tithes to God? The answer to that question is none. Jesus never said to give money unto God. As a matter of fact, He said give Caesar's money unto Caesar. Now let us look at tithes and offerings to God. No Gentile is able or ever was able to give tithes or offerings to God. Paul, who was sent to the Gentiles, referred to money as filthy lucre, and the Father stopped receiving tithes and offerings from the Jews since Amos 7:8 and 8:2. We look at Amos 7:8: "And the LORD said unto me, Amos, what seest thou? And I said a plumbline. Then said the LORD, Behold, I will set a plumbline in the midst of my people Israel: I will not again pass by them any more." There are

so many religious leaders who are compelling people to give money to God, something that cannot happen, but it is all a get-rich-quick scheme. The church today, which should be a body of believers converted and drawn to Jesus by the Father with one foundation and one shepherd, is referred to as a building. Hirelings (John 10:11–15) are putting too much money into buildings and bank accounts while the poor are being neglected. This is the same reason why Peter and the disciples appointed seven deacons—to see that certain members of the church (not a building) were not neglected.

> And in those days, when the number of the disciples was multiplied, there arose a murmuring of the Grecians against the Hebrews, because their widows were neglected in the daily ministration. Then the twelve called the multitude of the disciples unto them, and said, It is not reason that we should leave the word of God, and serve tables. Wherefore, brethren, look ye out among you seven men of honest report, full of the Holy Ghost and wisdom, whom we may appoint over this business. But we will give ourselves continually to prayer, and to the ministry of the word. And the saying pleased the whole multitude: and they chose Stephen, a man full of faith and of the Holy Ghost, and Philip, and Prochorus, and Nicanor, and Timon, and

> Parmenas, and Nicolas a proselyte of Antioch: Whom they set before the apostles: and when they had prayed, they laid their hands on them. (Acts 6:1–6)

From that time to now, the church has developed into a big business. Wayward leaders found the avenue of getting rich by building big buildings with the poor people's money using Malachi 10 (which never was and never will be for the Gentiles, and the Jews cannot even use it today) and lying to the people by saying the money is for God while they store it up in the bank and brag about it. All the hirelings have to do is have membership drive and tell people to come into the building, contrary to what Jesus said: "Go" (Matthew 28:19). They sit back and watch the money rolling in while the poor don't have food to eat. Jesus saw what they were doing and sent letters to them to get rid of those buildings and bank accounts, go out on the streets and to houses, and teach the Word without pay; remember, you cannot receive a reward from Jesus if you already received it down here. Let us take a look at one of the letters Jesus sent by John from the Isle of Patmos. In it Jesus told the church of the Laodiceans to get rid of those riches.

> Because thou sayest, I am rich, and increased with goods, and have need of nothing; and knowest not that thou art wretched, and miserable, and poor, and blind, and naked:

> I counsel thee to buy of me gold tried in the fire, that thou mayest be rich; and white raiment, that thou mayest be clothed, and that the shame of thy nakedness do not appear; and anoint thine eyes with eyesalve, that thou mayest see. (Revelation 3:17–18)

Why do the opposite of what Jesus is saying? Man is saying to come into the building; Jesus said to go into the fields for they are white to be harvest.

> Say not ye, There are yet four months, and then cometh harvest? Behold, I say unto you, Lift up your eyes, and look on the fields; for they are white already to harvest. And he that reapeth receiveth wages, and gathereth fruit unto life eternal: that both he that soweth and he that reapeth may rejoice together. And herein is that saying true, one soweth, and another reapeth. I sent you to reap that whereon ye bestowed no labour: other men laboured, and ye are entered into their labours. (John 4:35–38)

Matthew 9:38 says, "Pray ye therefore that the Father send laborers in the Harvest." The hirelings are praying that the Father will send members into the building illegally called the church. The harvest is not in a building. If Jesus said we cannot worship the Father in the Holy City, how can we worship in a building called church?

I know that it is hard for us to leave our comfort zones to go onto the hot, cold, and treacherous streets as did Jesus, His disciples, Paul, and the early Christians. I have met church people who said, "Come to the church. I don't have time now to talk on the streets." (I wonder if they would have said the same thing to the early church members.) When I got to the church, their time was limited. Would they have treated the Lord Jesus the same way? Maybe if they did not know who He was. Jesus set the example by walking the hot streets of Jerusalem and told us to do likewise. Jesus built the church; not by hands. Let us continue the journey of Jesus, His disciples, and Paul. Jesus said that you should not pray to the Father standing in synagogues and street corners as the hypocrites do to be seen of men. Why then it is done in the building called church? When Peter preached his first open-air sermon, three thousand souls were added to the church, not a building. Can you imagine over three thousand members in a building? I tell you; the hirelings would never let them go out. That would be a lot of money coming in. God forbid using His name to get rich; However, Jesus said that He will deal with those workers of iniquity. The Father also said He will deal with them.

> Woe be unto the pastors that destroy and scatter the sheep of my pasture! saith the LORD. Therefore thus saith the LORD God of Israel against the pastors that feed my people; Ye have scattered my flock, and driven them away, and have not visited them: behold, I will visit upon you the evil of your doings, saith the LORD. (Jeremiah 23:1–2)

Now let us look at some of the things Jesus wants us to do. The two main things are to believe that He is the Christ and to do what He tells us to do. Jesus said that whosoever lives and believes shall not die, but we must do the will of the Father. If we work for the Lord and do the will of the Father as commanded by Jesus, then we will not die when He returns. Matthew 12:50 says, "For whosoever shall do the will of my Father which is in heaven, the same is my brother, and sister, and mother." Matthew 16:27–28 says, "For the Son of man shall come in the glory of his Father with his angels; and then he shall reward every man according to his works. Verily I say unto you, there be some standing here, which shall not taste of death, till they see the Son of man coming in his kingdom."

Jesus has done all He possibly can for us. He has left the splendor of heaven, walked and talked with us, taught us how to live by not craving things of this world, having a loving, caring, giving, and forgiving heart, pardoned us of all our wrongdoings, gave us a paradise/heaven to rest in when we leave this earth, and instructed us that before we leave this earth, we must pray to the Father and ask the Father in Jesus' name to draw us unto Him so He will add our names to His list. If He put our name on His list (1John 5:7), when He returns from the Father, He will be able to put us on His right hand as sheep and take us to His Father's house. It is now up to us to heed His commandments so the Father will draw us unto Him. It is all left up to us. Remember that we have only a short time to do it. If you are able to do it now, do it. You do not have to speak out loud. The Father hears us from the heart; ask Him to draw you unto His Son, and let that be your daily prayer. Also ask for your family and friends to be drawn.

When the Father draws us, we will know and other people will see the changes.

The apostle Paul said in Romans 10:9, "That if thou shalt confess with thy mouth the Lord Jesus, and shalt believe in thine heart that God hath raised him from the dead, thou shalt be saved." (This is the first save; only the Father can second save you). Jesus wants us to keep His commandments in John 14:21: "He that hath my commandments, and keepeth them, he it is that loveth me: and he that loveth me shall be loved of my Father, and I will love him, and will manifest myself to him." Remember, Jesus said to go to the Father in His name. John 14:6 says, "Jesus saith unto him, I am the way, the truth, and the life: no man cometh unto the Father, but by me." This Scripture means two things: (1) you must go to the Father in Jesus' name, and (2) only Jesus can take you to the Father. Remember also, Jesus said that no one can come to Him except the Father draw him. As it says in John 6:45 and 65,

> It is written in the prophets, and they shall be all taught of God. Every man therefore that hath heard, and hath learned of the Father, cometh unto me… And he said, therefore said I unto you, that no man can come unto me, except it were given unto him of my Father.

Jesus also commanded us to let our works be seen of men so they may give glory to God in Matthew 5:16: "Let your light so shine before men, that they may see your good works, and glorify your Father which is in heaven." Moses gave the commandment on the subject of divorce, and Jesus made it null and void. With no offense to Mosses, Jesus knew that Moses did what was best at that time. Here is what Jesus said to the Pharisees when they asked him about divorce:

> And he answered and said unto them, Have ye not read, that he which made them at the beginning made them male and female, And said, For this cause shall a man leave father and mother, and shall cleave to his wife: and they twain shall be one flesh? Wherefore they are no more twain, but one flesh. What therefore God hath joined together, let not man put asunder. They say unto him, why did Moses then command to give a writing of divorcement, and to put her away? He saith unto them, Moses because of the hardness of your hearts suffered you to put away your wives: but from the beginning it was not so. And I say unto you, whosoever shall put away his wife, except it be for fornication, and shall marry another, committeth adultery: and whoso marrieth her which is put away doth commit adultery. (Matthew 19:4–9)

> What therefore God hath joined together, let not man put asunder. And in the house his disciples asked him again of the same matter. And he saith unto them, whosoever shall put away his wife, and marry another, committeth adultery against her. (Mark 10:9–11)

There is no way we can get around it. In the beginning the Father said, "Let not man put it asunder"; who then wants to explain to the Father God why He was disobeyed? Jesus said do not put your wife away for any cause except fornication, which means an engaged or espoused couple, who should be virgins, like unto His mother Mary when she was found with child of the Holy Ghost, which is God. Matthew 1:18 says, "Now the birth of Jesus Christ was on this wise: When as his mother Mary was espoused to Joseph, before they came together, she was found with child of the Holy Ghost." In the days of Jesus, engaged couples were referred to as husband and wife. What Jesus is saying in Matthew 19:9 is if this wife fornicates, put her away. There will be no more women impregnated by the Holy Ghost, and there is no more Jesus to come. Therefore if any virgin says she is pregnant, it is not so. She has fornicated. Therefore put her away and be married to another. That is the only legal course for divorce.

Should all women heed God's Word and abide in Genesis 3:16, there would be no need for divorce; Genesis 3:16 says, "Unto the woman he said, I will greatly multiply thy sorrow and thy conception; in sorrow thou shalt bring forth children; and thy desire shall be to thy husband, and he shall rule over thee." You cannot be of the world and of God. He wants to second save you and draw you unto His Son. John 6:44 says, "No man can come to me, except the Father which hath sent me draw him: and I will raise him up at the last day." Should the Father not draw you unto His Son, when Jesus comes back from the Father's heaven to the third heaven/paradise, He will not be able to put you on His right as sheep and take you to the Father, as Matthew 25:31–34 Says,

> When the Son of man shall come in his glory, and all the holy angels with him, then shall he sit upon the throne of his glory: And before him shall be gathered all nations: and he shall separate them one from another, as a shepherd divideth his sheep from the goats: And he shall set the sheep on his right hand, but the goats on the left. Then shall the King say unto them on his right hand, Come, ye blessed of my Father, inherit the kingdom prepared for you from the foundation of the world:

I conclude with this prayer that you have understood and the Lord will use you in His harvest to teach others about His Word amen. God bless you.

(2)

Are You a Jew or a Gentile?

What is the origin of the Jews, and who are Gentiles? Let us have a look at what the King James Version (KJV) of the Bible says. First we want to understand that Jews are God's chosen people who worshipped Him in the way that He requested, and Gentiles are all those who are not Jews who worshipped other gods and were out of favor with God. After the Lord had destroyed the earth by water and rebeautified it, He told Noah to send his three sons and their wives to replenish the earth. We want to note that Japheth was sent to the Gentiles.

> These are the generations of the sons of Noah, Shem, Ham, and Japheth: and unto them were sons born after the flood. The sons of Japheth (were); Gomer, and Magog, and Madai, and Javan, and Tubal, and Meshech, and Tiras … By these were the isles of the Gentiles divided in their lands; every one after his tongue, after their families, in their nations … These are the families of the sons

> of Noah, after their generations, in their nations: and by these were the nations divided in the earth after the flood. (Genesis 10:1–2, 5, 32)

Noah's children were closely knitted, and they refused to spread out into the world; therefore God confounded their language so they were compelled to go into the entire world. In the next Scripture we understand that Abram/Abraham (father of the Jews) came through the lineage of Shem.

> And the whole earth was of one language, and of one speech. And it came to pass, as they journeyed from the east, that they found a plain in the land of Shinar; and they dwelt there. And they said one to another, Go to, let us make brick, and burn them thoroughly. And they had brick for stone, and slime had they for morter. And they said, Go to, let us build us a city and a tower, whose top may reach unto heaven; and let us make us a name, lest we be scattered abroad upon the face of the whole earth. And the LORD came down to see the city and the tower, which the children of men builded. And the LORD said, Behold, the people is one, and they have all one language; and this they begin to do: and now nothing will be restrained from them, which they have imagined to do. Go to, let us go down, and there confound their language, that they may not understand one another's speech. So the LORD scattered them abroad from thence

> upon the face of all the earth: and they left off to build the city. Therefore is the name of it called Babel; because the LORD did there confound the language of all the earth: and from thence did the LORD scatter them abroad upon the face of all the earth. These are **the generations of** Shem: Shem was an hundred years old, and begat Arphaxad two years after the flood. [My understanding is that Abram was the son of Terah and the Jews came through Noah's son, Shem.] … Now these are the generations of Terah: Terah begat Abram, Nahor, and Haran; and Haran begat Lot. And Haran died before his father Terah in the land of his nativity, in Ur of the Chaldees. (Genesis 11:1–10, 27–28, emphasis added)

After the flood and replenishment of the earth, long after Noah died, people on the earth again turned away from God, all except Abram and his nephew, Lot. As we see in the next Scripture, God told Abram to leave his father's house and that He would give him a land (Israel) and make him a great nation (Jews), and through him all families would be blessed. (Because all families are blessed through Abram does not make them Jews.) We see in the next Scripture that the Father God said that whosoever blesses or curses Israel, He will bless or curse them. This is the beginning of the Jews.

> Now the LORD had said unto Abram, Get thee out of thy country, and from thy kindred, and from

> thy father›s house, unto a land that I will shew thee: And I will make of thee a great nation, and I will bless thee, and make thy name great; and thou shalt be a blessing: And I will bless them that bless thee, and curse him that curseth thee: and in thee shall all families of the earth be blessed. So Abram departed, as the LORD had spoken unto him; and Lot went with him: and Abram was seventy and five years old when he departed out of Haran. (Genesis 12:1–4)

Let us ponder upon this; when Abram left his father's house with his wife, Sarai, and nephew, Lot, he was seventy-five years old and did not have a child of his own. When Abram was ninety-nine years old, God made the covenant of circumcision with Abram, changed his and his wife's name from Abram to Abraham and from Sarai to Sarah, and promised him that he would have a son, Isaac, in the next year at age one hundred. Note in Genesis 16:3 at this time Abraham had already married his wife's handmaid, Hagar (an Egyptian who was a Gentile), who gave him a son called Ishmael. The Lord said He would make a great nation of Ishmael but not the Jewish nation and that He would establish His covenant with Isaac.

> And when Abram was ninety years old and nine, the LORD appeared to Abram, and said unto him, I am the Almighty God; walk before me, and be thou perfect. And I will make my covenant between me and thee, and will multiply thee

exceedingly. And Abram fell on his face: and God talked with him, saying, As for me, behold, my covenant is with thee, and thou shalt be a father of many nations. Neither shall thy name any more be called Abram, but thy name shall be Abraham; for a father of many nations have I made thee. And I will make thee exceeding fruitful, and I will make nations of thee, and kings shall come out of thee. And I will establish my covenant between me and thee and thy seed after thee in their generations for an everlasting covenant, to be a God unto thee, and to thy seed after thee. And I will give unto thee and to thy seed after thee, the land wherein thou art a stranger, all the land of Canaan, for an everlasting possession; and I will be their God. And God said unto Abraham, Thou shalt keep my covenant therefore, thou, and thy seed after thee in their generations. This is my covenant, which ye shall keep, between me and you and thy seed after thee; every man child among you shall be circumcised. And ye shall circumcise the flesh of your foreskin; and it shall be a token of the covenant betwixt me and you. And he that is eight days old shall be circumcised among you, every man child in your generations, he that is born in the house, or bought with money of any stranger, which is not of thy seed. He that is born in thy house, and he that is bought with thy money, must

> needs be circumcised: and my covenant shall be in your flesh for an everlasting covenant. And the uncircumcised man child whose flesh of his foreskin is not circumcised, that soul shall be cut off from his people; he hath broken my covenant. And God said unto Abraham, As for Sarai thy wife, thou shalt not call her name Sarai, but Sarah shall her name be. And I will bless her, and give thee a son also of her: yea, I will bless her, and she shall be a mother of nations; kings of people shall be of her. Then Abraham fell upon his face, and laughed, and said in his heart, Shall a child be born unto him that is an hundred years old? and shall Sarah, that is ninety years old, bear? And Abraham said unto God, O that Ishmael might live before thee! And God said, Sarah thy wife shall bear thee a son indeed; and thou shalt call his name Isaac: and I will establish my covenant with him for an everlasting covenant, and with his seed after him. And as for Ishmael, I have heard thee: Behold, I have blessed him, and will make him fruitful, and will multiply him exceedingly; twelve princes shall he beget, and I will make him a great nation. But my covenant will I establish with Isaac, which Sarah shall bear unto thee at this set time in the next year. (Genesis 17:1–21)

We want to understand here that Isaac and his wife, Rebekah, had twin boys, and the Lord said that they are two nations, two separate people, one stronger than the other, and the elder (Esau) shall serve the younger (Jacob). Therefore Jacob got his father's blessing, and he became the Jewish nation.

> And Isaac entreated the LORD for his wife, because she was barren: and the LORD was entreated of him, and Rebekah his wife conceived. And the children struggled together within her; and she said, if it be so, why am I thus? And she went to enquire of the LORD. And the LORD said unto her, two nations are in thy womb, and two manner of people shall be separated from thy bowels; and the one people shall be stronger than the other people; and the elder shall serve the younger. And when her days to be delivered were fulfilled, behold, there were twins in her womb. And the first came out red, all over like a hairy garment; and they called his name Esau. And after that came his brother out, and his hand took hold on Esau's heel; and his name was called Jacob: and Isaac was threescore years old when she bare them. (Genesis 25:21–26)

Some points to note here; father, son, and grandson (Abraham, Isaac, and Jacob) all had to pray to God for their beloved wives to have a child, and none of their firstborn received their father's blessings from God. Abraham's wife Sarah was barren, Isaac's wife, Rebekah, was barren, and Jacob's beloved wife Rachel was barren. God blessed them all with children in their late years.

Abraham's blessings went to his second son, Isaac; Isaac's blessing went to his second son, Jacob; and Jacob's blessings went to his eleventh son, Joseph, by whom the nation of Israel went into Egypt, where they became slaves for four hundred years.

> And God remembered Rachel, and God hearkened to her, and opened her womb. And she conceived, and bare a son; and said, God hath taken away my reproach: and she called his name Joseph; and said, The LORD shall add to me another son. And it came to pass, when Rachel had born Joseph, that Jacob said unto Laban, Send me away, that I may go unto mine own place, and to my country. (Genesis 30:22–25)

When Jacob left his uncle Laban (his mother Rebekah's brother), who was also his father-in-law (Leah and Rachael's father), on his way to the Promised Land, we see that he wrestled with God and God changed his name from Jacob to Israel; this is where the Jews became Israelites.

> And Jacob was left alone; and there wrestled a man with him until the breaking of the day. And when he saw that he prevailed not against him, he touched the hollow of his thigh; and the hollow of Jacob's thigh was out of joint, as he wrestled with him. And he said, let me go, for the day breaketh. And he said, I will not let thee go, except thou bless me. And he said unto him, what is thy name?

> And he said, Jacob. And he said, Thy name shall be called no more Jacob, but Israel: for as a prince hast thou power with God and with men, and hast prevailed. (Genesis 32:24–28)

Jacob's wife Rachael had two sons, Joseph and Benjamin, the last two sons who made up the twelve tribes of Israel. Rachael died while giving birth to Benjamin. Joseph, who was not loved by his brothers because of his dreams, was sold into Egypt as a slave. Because of Joseph's devotion to God while in Egypt, he was cast into a dungeon. Then the pharaoh of Egypt had a very troubling dream that none of his intelligent men were able to give the interpretation of. When the pharaoh heard about Joseph the dreamer, he sent for him and told him about the dream. When Joseph told the pharaoh what the dream meant, the pharaoh gave Joseph a very high position in Egypt, next only to the pharaoh.

> Then Pharaoh sent and called Joseph, and they brought him hastily out of the dungeon: and he shaved himself, and changed his raiment, and came in unto Pharaoh. And Pharaoh said unto Joseph, I have dreamed a dream, and there is none that can interpret it: and I have heard say of thee, that thou canst understand a dream to interpret it. And Joseph answered Pharaoh, saying, It is not in me: God shall give Pharaoh an answer of peace. And Pharaoh said unto Joseph, In my dream, behold, I stood upon the bank of the river: And, behold, there came up out of the

river seven kine, fatfleshed and well favoured; and they fed in a meadow: And, behold, seven other kine came up after them, poor and very ill favoured and leanfleshed, such as I never saw in all the land of Egypt for badness: And the lean and the ill favoured kine did eat up the first seven fat kine: And when they had eaten them up, it could not be known that they had eaten them; but they were still ill favoured, as at the beginning. So I awoke. And I saw in my dream, and, behold, seven ears came up in one stalk, full and good: And, behold, seven ears, withered, thin, and blasted with the east wind, sprung up after them: And the thin ears devoured the seven good ears: and I told this unto the magicians; but there was none that could declare it to me. And Joseph said unto Pharaoh, The dream of Pharaoh is one: God hath shewed Pharaoh what he is about to do. The seven good kine are seven years; and the seven good ears are seven years: the dream is one. And the seven thin and ill favoured kine that came up after them are seven years; and the seven empty ears blasted with the east wind shall be seven years of famine. This is the thing which I have spoken unto Pharaoh: What God is about to do he sheweth unto Pharaoh. Behold, there come seven years of great plenty throughout all the land of Egypt: And there shall arise after them seven years of famine; and all the plenty shall be forgotten in the land of Egypt; and the famine shall consume the land; And the plenty shall not be known in the land by reason of that famine following; for it shall be very grievous. And for that the dream was doubled unto Pharaoh twice; it is because the thing is established by God, and God will shortly bring it to pass. Now therefore let Pharaoh look out a man discreet and wise, and set him over the land of Egypt. Let Pharaoh do this, and let him appoint officers over the land, and take up the fifth part of the land of Egypt in the seven plenteous years. And let them gather all the food of those good years that come, and lay up corn under the hand of Pharaoh, and let them keep food in the cities. And that food shall be for store to the land against the seven years of famine, which shall be in the land of Egypt; that the land perish not through the famine. And the thing was good in the eyes of Pharaoh, and in the eyes of all his servants. And Pharaoh said unto his servants, Can we find such a one as this is, a man in whom the Spirit of God is? And Pharaoh said unto Joseph, Forasmuch as God hath shewed thee all this, there is none so discreet and wise as thou art: Thou shalt be over my house, and according unto thy word shall all my people be ruled: only in the throne will I be greater than thou. And Pharaoh said unto Joseph, See, I have set thee over all the land of Egypt. And Pharaoh

> took off his ring from his hand, and put it upon Joseph's hand, and arrayed him in vestures of fine linen, and put a gold chain about his neck; And he made him to ride in the second chariot which he had; and they cried before him, Bow the knee: and he made him ruler over all the land of Egypt. (Genesis 41:14–43)

Now because of the great famine and because only Egypt had grain, Joseph's brothers who sold him into Egypt had to go to him for rations. It had been such a long time that they did not even recognize him, but Joseph knew who they were. He wanted to see his youngest brother, Benjamin, and his dad, Jacob-Israel, who was very old at that time. After Joseph revealed himself to his brothers and the pharaoh heard of them, he was pleased and provided wagons for Joseph to bring all the Israelites into Egypt. The Lord spoke to Jacob in a dream and told him to take the children of Israel into Egypt so Joseph should see him before he died and that the Lord would be with them and lead them out again.

> And Israel took his journey with all that he had, and came to Beersheba, and offered sacrifices unto the God of his father Isaac. And God spake unto Israel in the visions of the night, and said, Jacob, Jacob. And he said, Here am I. And he said, I am God, the God of thy father: fear not to go down into Egypt; for I will there make of thee a great nation: I will go down with thee into Egypt; and I will also surely bring thee up again: and Joseph

> shall put his hand upon thine eyes. And Jacob rose up from Beersheba: and the sons of Israel carried Jacob their father, and their little ones, and their wives, in the wagons which Pharaoh had sent to carry him. And they took their cattle, and their goods, which they had gotten in the land of Canaan, and came into Egypt, Jacob, and all his seed with him … The sons of Rachel Jacob's wife; Joseph, and Benjamin. And unto Joseph in the land of Egypt were born Manasseh and Ephraim, which Asenath the daughter of Potipherah priest of On bare unto him. (Genesis 46:1–6 and 19–20)

Joseph made the children of Israel take an oath that they would take his bones into the Promised Land.

> And Joseph said unto his brethren, I die: and God will surely visit you, and bring you out of this land unto the land which he sware to Abraham, to Isaac, and to Jacob. And Joseph took an oath of the children of Israel, saying, God will surely visit you, and ye shall carry up my bones from hence. So Joseph died, being an hundred and ten years old: and they embalmed him, and he was put in a coffin in Egypt. (Genesis 50:24–26)

Now after Joseph died and a new pharaoh ruled who knew nothing of the good that Joseph had done, he made the Israelites slaves, just as the Lord told Abraham that He would send his seed into bondage for four hundred years. The following Scripture is a reminder of what God said to Abraham. It also says no Gentiles can eat of the Passover supper, and Moses fulfilled Joseph's request to be buried in the Promised Land.

> And he said unto Abram, Know of a surety that thy seed shall be a stranger in a land that is not theirs, and shall serve them; and they shall afflict them four hundred years; And also that nation, whom they shall serve, will I judge: and afterward shall they come out with great substance. (Genesis 15:13–14)

> And it came to pass at the end of the four hundred and thirty years, even the selfsame day it came to pass, that all the hosts of the LORD went out from the land of Egypt. It is a night to be much observed unto the LORD for bringing them out from the land of Egypt: this is that night of the LORD to be observed of all the children of Israel in their generations. And the LORD said unto Moses and Aaron, This is the ordinance of the Passover: There shall no stranger eat thereof: But every man's servant that is bought for money, when thou hast circumcised him, then shall he eat thereof. A foreigner and an hired servant shall not eat thereof. (Exodus 12:41–45)

> And Moses took the bones of Joseph with him: for he had straitly sworn the children of Israel, saying, God will surely visit you; and ye shall carry up my bones away hence with you. (Exodus 13:19)

The following Scripture stipulates the land of Israel, which the Lord told Abraham that He gave unto the children of Israel. I don't think the Jews had ever occupied all of it. Genesis 15:18 says, "In the same day the LORD made a covenant with Abram, saying, Unto thy seed have I given this land, from the river of Egypt unto the great river, the river Euphrates."

We see that Moses led the children of Israel out of Egypt through the waters on dry land. The Lord allowed Moses to see the Holy City but not to enter in. Joshua, who succeeded Moses, also took the children through waters on dry land before they entered the city. We will also see in the Scriptures below that Joshua forewarned the children of Israel before they entered into the city that they and their children to come must keep God's commandments. As we see, the children turned away from God, and He forsook them.

> And Moses stretched out his hand over the sea; and the LORD caused the sea to go back by a strong east wind all that night, and made the sea dry land, and the waters were divided. And the children of Israel went into the midst of the sea upon the dry ground: and the waters were a wall unto them on their right hand, and on their left. (Exodus 14:21–22)

And it came to pass, when the people removed from their tents, to pass over Jordan, and the priests bearing the ark of the covenant before the people; And as they that bare the ark were come unto Jordan, and the feet of the priests that bare the ark were dipped in the brim of the water, (for Jordan overfloweth all his banks all the time of harvest,) That the waters which came down from above stood and rose up upon an heap very far from the city Adam, that is beside Zaretan: and those that came down toward the sea of the plain, even the salt sea, failed, and were cut off: and the people passed over right against Jericho. And the priests that bare the ark of the covenant of the LORD stood firm on dry ground in the midst of Jordan, and all the Israelites passed over on dry ground, until all the people were passed clean over Jordan. (Joshua 3:14–17)

Now these are the commandments, the statutes, and the judgments, which the LORD your God commanded to teach you, that ye might do them in the land whither ye go to possess it: That thou mightest fear the LORD thy God, to keep all his statutes and his commandments, which I command thee, thou, and thy son, and thy son's son, all the days of thy life; and that thy days may be prolonged. Hear therefore, O Israel, and observe to do it; that it may be well with thee, and that ye may increase mightily, as the LORD God of thy fathers hath promised thee, in the land that floweth with milk and honey. (Deuteronomy 6:1–3)

Now Jericho was straitly shut up because of the children of Israel: none went out, and none came in. And the LORD said unto Joshua, See, I have given into thine hand Jericho, and the king thereof, and the mighty men of valour … And it came to pass on the seventh day, that they rose early about the dawning of the day, and compassed the city after the same manner seven times: only on that day they compassed the city seven times. And it came to pass at the seventh time, when the priests blew with the trumpets, Joshua said unto the people, Shout; for the LORD hath given you the city. (Joshua 6:1–2, 15–16)

Neither have our kings, our princes, our priests, nor our fathers, kept thy law, nor hearkened unto thy commandments and thy testimonies, wherewith thou didst testify against them. For they have not served thee in their kingdom, and in thy great goodness that thou gavest them, and in the large and fat land which thou gavest before them, neither turned they from their wicked works. (Nehemiah 9:34–35)

> Therefore, behold, I, even I, will utterly forget you, and I will forsake you, and the city that I gave you and your fathers, and cast you out of my presence. (Jeremiah 23:39)

> And the Lord said unto me, Amos, what seest thou? And I said, A plumbline. Then said the Lord, Behold, I will set a plumbline in the midst of my people Israel: I will not again pass by them any more. (Amos 7:8)

> And he said, Amos, what seest thou? And I said, A basket of summer fruit. Then said the Lord unto me, the end is come upon my people of Israel; I will not again pass by them anymore. (Amos 8:2)

Here is what I have to say: Father God has never again gone into the temple of the Jews (Holy of Holies) to receive more tithes and offerings. In the same way the Lord rejected Cain's offering, He has rejected the Jews' offerings. However, because of the veil that separated the people from the altar (where God had received the offerings), there was no way the people could have known that the Lord did not receive the sacrifices. Therefore the priests pretended as if the heavenly Father was receiving the sacrifices. When Jesus Christ the Messiah came to the Jews, not the Gentiles, He told them that they could no longer worship the Father anywhere in the Holy City, not even in a building. Remember, David, the king of Israel, wanted to build a temple for the Lord, but the Father rejected him. Do you think He would allow a Gentile who is not in the law of God (Romans 2:14) to build a house unto Him? Of course not. Read what Jesus said to the woman at the well of Samaria who thought she was a Jew.

Jesus saith unto her, Woman, believe me, the hour cometh, when ye shall neither in this mountain, nor yet at Jerusalem, worship the Father. Ye worship ye know not what: we know what we worship: for salvation is of the Jews. But the hour cometh and now is, when the true worshippers shall worship the Father in spirit and in truth: for the Father seeketh such to worship him. God is a Spirit: and they that worship him must worship him in spirit and in truth. (John 4:21–24)

One of Jesus' disciples showed Him the beautiful stones of the temple. Here is what Jesus said to him:

> And Jesus answering said unto him, Seest thou these great buildings? There shall not be left one stone upon another that shall not be thrown down. (Mark 13:2)

Right now in the year 2014 the temple is no more, and a mosque is built on that site. Why are men ignoring Jesus' words and deceiving many people that they can still worship the Father in a building or anywhere other than in spirit and in truth, from the heart, as Jesus said?

> This people draweth nigh unto me with their mouth, and honoureth me with their lips; but their

> heart is far from me. But in vain they do worship me, teaching for doctrines the commandments of men. (Matthew 15:8–9)

When Jesus was on the cross (we know it was a cross and not a torture stake, as some men say, because after Jesus rode the donkey through the streets of Jerusalem on the way to be crucified. The mark of the cross has ever since been seen on the back of all thoroughbred donkeys.) After He said, "It is finished," the veil of the temple was rent from top to bottom so that all the people could see for themselves that no more sacrifices were being received by God. Jesus said in His Word that the Father is seeking true worshippers to worship Him from the heart so the Father may draw them unto Jesus, as understood in John.

> No man can come to me, except the Father which hath sent me draw him: and I will raise him up at the last day. It is written in the prophets, and they shall be all taught of God. Every man therefore that hath heard, and hath learned of the Father, cometh unto me … And he said, therefore said I unto you, that no man can come unto me, except it were given unto him of my Father. (John 6:44–45, 65)

We must understand that everyone; be you Jew or Gentile, must be converted to Christianity by the Father (Matthew 18:3, Luke 22:31–32). We must ask the Father to draw us unto His Son in Jesus' name so He will take us to the Father.

Let us look at this statement that is often misunderstood. Jesus is speaking to Thomas in John 14:6: "Jesus saith unto him, I am the way, the truth, and the life: no man cometh unto the Father, but by me."

This statement means two things: (1) only in the name of Jesus can anyone go to the Father to be saved, and (2) only Jesus can take you to the Father. Once the Father draws you unto the Son, you are saved forevermore.

> My sheep hear my voice, and I know them, and they follow me: And I give unto them eternal life; and they shall never perish, neither shall any man pluck them out of my hand. My Father, which gave them me, is greater than all; and no man is able to pluck them out of my Father's hand. (John 10:27–29)

I leave these words with you that Paul gave to the Romans, who are also Gentiles:

> Now I say that Jesus Christ was a minister of the circumcision for the truth of God, to confirm the promises made unto the fathers: And that the Gentiles might glorify God for his mercy; as it is written, For this cause I will confess to thee among the Gentiles, and sing unto thy name … Nevertheless, brethren, I have written the more boldly unto you in some sort, as putting you in mind, because of the grace that is given to me

> of God, That I should be the minister of Jesus Christ to the Gentiles, ministering the gospel of God, that the offering up of the Gentiles might be acceptable, being sanctified by the Holy Ghost. (Romans 15:8–9 and 15–16)

In conclusion, to make it simple, a Jew is a circumcised male and anyone born or bought in the Jewish family. All others are Gentiles. We must remember that Jews and Gentiles must be converted to Christianity by the Father God through His Holy Ghost to be taken by the Son to the Father. Believe that Jesus is the Son of God and tell others of God's invitation to them so they may come into His kingdom before He sets this earth ablaze.

> The first angel sounded, and there followed hail and fire mingled with blood, and they were cast upon the earth: and the third part of trees was burnt up, and all green grass was burnt up … And I beheld, and heard an angel flying through the midst of heaven, saying with a loud voice, Woe, woe, woe, to the inhabiters of the earth by reason of the other voices of the trumpet of the three angels, which are yet to sound! (Revelation 8:7, 13)

Jew or Gentile, we do not want to remain on this earth. God bless you.

(3)

The Greatest Religious Question

Before I go into this message, I must tell you about the three heavens and the two saves, which I explained briefly earlier. It is very important for you to know, remember, and teach people about the three heavens and the two saves. For all people you speak to about this message, will not understand it until they learn about them. They should have a clear picture of where they will go when they leave this earth and what they must do to get there. Jesus is depending on you, Matthew 28:19.

We understand from the book of Genesis that there are three heavens, the first being the heaven where the Father dwells. People often say that when we leave this earth, we will go to be with the Lord. We should not believe that. We will not go to the Father until we are taken there by Jesus Christ, the Son of God. Here is what John said in John 3:13: "And no man hath ascended up to heaven, but he that came down from heaven, even the Son of man which is in heaven." The second heaven is where the sun, moon, and stars are to give light to the earth. The third heaven is between the sea and the clouds, where the birds fly. Jesus called it paradise; this is where the saved people are, all who believe that Jesus Christ is the Messiah and the Son of God. They will tarry there until Jesus returns to gather the Saints. All who do not believe will not go to paradise but find themselves in hell, as we see in John 3:18: "He that believeth on him is not condemned: but he that believeth not is condemned already, because he hath not believed in the name of the only begotten Son of God."

We must understand that there are two saves. Matthew 16:28 says, "Verily I say unto you, there be some standing here, which shall not taste of death, till they see the Son of man coming in his kingdom." There are those who only believe but have not gone to the Father in prayer in Jesus' name to ask the Father to draw them unto His Son that they may be converted by the Father. If they are not drawn to Jesus, they will die when Jesus returns from the first heaven to the third heaven. Then there are those who believe and obey the words of the Lord Jesus and are converted and drawn unto Him by the Father. These are those who are saved forevermore. Jesus will put them on His right hand as sheep when He returns to paradise-His temporary Kingdom. Therefore we see in this next Scripture John said that if we only believe on Jesus' name we are saved, but that salvation will not get us to the Father's heaven. It only gives us power to become the sons of God. (I want to remind you here that Jesus was first sent unto His own people the Jews, then to the Gentiles.)

> He came unto his own, and his own received him not. But as many as received him, to them gave he power to become the sons of God, even to them that believe on his name. (John 1:11–12)

The first save you can become unsaved by changing your mind and not believing that Jesus is the Son of God. For the second save, as seen in John, Jesus said only the Father can second save you by drawing you unto Him, and He will raise you up at the last day and give you eternal life. John 6:44 says, "No man can come to me, except the Father which hath sent me draw him: and I will raise him up at the last day." Once the Father has saved you, there is no looking back; you are saved forevermore.

> My sheep hear my voice, and I know them, and they follow me: And I give unto them eternal life; and they shall never perish, neither shall any man pluck them out of my hand. My Father, which gave them me, is greater than all; and no man is able to pluck them out of my Father's hand. (John 10:27–29)

Now that we understand the three heavens and two saves, we go to the question of the day.

The greatest religious question: Why are believers like kings, popes, priests, bishops, false prophets, pastors, presidents, prime ministers, and politicians going to the third heaven/paradise but are not sure if they will be taken by Jesus to the first heaven, God's kingdom? This question can only be answered by the individual; are you prepared to give up all power and riches for the kingdom of God? Let us go into the word of God.

Pope and priest: A pope is at the highest order of the Gentiles' religious faith (all who believes that Jesus Christ is the Son of God), not so in the body of Christ (all who the Father has drawn unto the Son), and there is no affiliation with the Jews. A priest, as we understand, is unto the Jews, and the Father was not too happy with them; and in the body of Christ, no man should be called a priest.

Here is what the Father said to His people, the Jews:

> For both prophet and priest are profane; yea, in my house have I found their wickedness, saith the Lord … And as for the prophet, and the priest, and the people, that shall say, The burden of the Lord, I will even punish that man and his house. (Jeremiah 23:11, 34)

Here is what Jesus said to the Jews and by extension the Gentiles in Matthew 23:9: "And call no man your father upon the earth: for one is your Father, which is in heaven." I must comment on this; oftentimes I hear men finding their own justification, ratification, or elimination of Jesus' sayings to fulfill their own purpose. The Word of God is to either be rejected and left alone or accepted, where we allow the Holy Spirit to give the understanding of it. Here is what Jesus said to His disciples when He was about to leave this world:

> And I will pray the Father, and he shall give you another Comforter, that he may abide with you forever … But the Comforter, which is the Holy Ghost, whom the Father will send in my name, he shall teach you all things, and bring all things to your remembrance, whatsoever I have said unto you. (John 14:16 and 26)

Jesus told His disciples not to be called any name higher than brethren.

> But Jesus called them unto him, and said, Ye know that the princes of the Gentiles exercise dominion over them, and they that are great exercise authority upon them. But it shall not be so among you: but whosoever will be great among you, let him be your minister; And whosoever will be chief among you, let him be your servant: Even as the Son of man came not to be ministered unto, but to minister, and to give his life a ransom for many. (Matthew 20:25–28)

That Scripture made it clear as day—popes, priests, fathers, and other titles like these are names that should not be used in the body of Christ. We must obey the sayings of the Lord Jesus if we really love Him. Let us not be like the Jews, who said they loved the Father but would not obey His words. The Jews are God's chosen people, which do not include anyone who is not an Israelite. They were always in and out of favor with God until God said that He would forsake them and not pass by them anymore, as we see in Jeremiah 23:39–40, Amos 7:8, and Amos 8:2 (Quoted earlier in this book).

Wayward prophets and false prophets: All who understand the Word of God will not call themselves prophets at this time. The entire chapter of Jeremiah 23 explains God's anger toward false and wayward prophets. Jeremiah 23:9 tells about the actions of the prophets and the harsh words the Lord spoke unto them that made

Jeremiah very sick: "Mine heart within me is broken because of the prophets; all my bones shake; I am like a drunken man, and like a man whom wine hath overcome, because of the LORD, and because of the words of his holiness." It is good for us to note here that the Samaritans, who thought they were Jews, had false prophets who they thought were real prophets and even persuaded some Jews to believe in them. Jeremiah 23:13 says, "And I have seen folly in the prophets of Samaria; they prophesied in Baal, and caused my people Israel to err." Here is what God said about His Prophets that went wayward. Jeremiah 23:16 says, "Thus saith the LORD of hosts, Hearken not unto the words of the prophets that prophesy unto you: they make you vain: they speak a vision of their own heart, and not out of the mouth of the LORD." The Lord God said in Jeremiah 23:11–12 that both prophets and priests would continue their wickedness in His house until the Lord Jesus came to the Jews.

> For both prophet and priest are profane; yea, in my house have I found their wickedness, saith the LORD. Wherefore their way shall be unto them as slippery ways in the darkness: they shall be driven on, and fall therein: for I will bring evil upon them, even the year of their visitation, saith the LORD. (Jeremiah 23:11–12)

When Jesus came (visitation) to the Jews, He put an end to real prophets coming to earth. John the Baptist was the last real prophet. Luke 16:16 says, "The law and the prophets were until John: since that time the kingdom of God is preached, and every man presseth into it." And Matthew 11:12–13 says, "And from the days of John the Baptist until now the kingdom of heaven suffereth violence, and the violent take it by force. For all the prophets and the law prophesied until John." All other prophets are false prophets.

Let me explain to you this statement: "The kingdom of heaven suffereth violence, and the violent take it by force." When John the Baptist began to preach (Matthew 3:2) to the Jews, telling them to repent for the kingdom of God was at hand, the Jews found it hard to put away the Law to abide in the gospel. Therefore they rebelled against John's and Jesus' words (the kingdom of God/gospel), and up to now the Jews and even other factions are fighting against the gospel. They refused to give up prophets. However, Jesus admonished us to be aware of false prophets: "Beware of false prophets, which come to you in sheep's clothing, but inwardly they are ravening wolves" (Matthew 7:15).

Pastors and bishops: What can any man say that can supersede the words of the heavenly Father and His Son? The Father said that only He appoints pastors according to His heart, and Jesus told His disciples not to be called anything above brethren, as we see in the Scriptures below. The apostle Paul referred to the Law in Jeremiah when he wrote Ephesians 4:11, but apparently he was not aware that Jesus said that the Law was until John the Baptist. I believe that the apostle Paul, a servant of God, did not want his teachings to override, question, or eradicate the teachings of the Lord Jesus. This Scripture in Jeremiah tells us that only the Father gives pastors, as Paul said, but this is under the Law and only for Jews, not Gentiles.

> And he gave some, apostles; and some, prophets; and some, evangelists; and some, pastors and teachers. (Ephesians 4:11)

> And I will give you pastors according to mine heart, which shall feed you with knowledge and understanding. Jesus said that the law ended with John the Baptist. (Jeremiah 3:15)

> The law and the prophets were until John: since that time the kingdom of God is preached, and every man presseth into it. (Luke 16:16)

Understand that a pastor is a person who calls himself or herself a shepherd of the sheep. However the Father said that He will recompense evil unto them. Jesus called them hirelings (those who are paid to do a job) and not the shepherd of His sheep. Let us look at the Scriptures.

> Woe be unto the pastors that destroy and scatter the sheep of my pasture! saith the LORD. Therefore thus saith the LORD God of Israel against the pastors that feed my people; Ye have scattered my flock, and driven them away, and have not visited them: behold, I will visit upon you the evil of your doings, saith the LORD. (Jeremiah 23:1–2)

> [Jesus said] I am the good shepherd: the good shepherd giveth his life for the sheep. But he that is

> an hireling, and not the shepherd, whose own the sheep are not, seeth the wolf coming, and leaveth the sheep, and fleeth: and the wolf catcheth them, and scattereth the sheep. The hireling fleeth, because he is an hireling, and careth not for the sheep. I am the good shepherd, and know my sheep, and am known of mine. As the Father knoweth me, even so know I the Father: and I lay down my life for the sheep. (John 10:11–15)

It is often said that the apostle Paul appointed bishops, but that is not so. In Paul's letter to Timothy, we get the understanding that Timothy informed Paul of the people's desire to appoint bishops. However, Paul was not aware of Jesus' command that all of His followers be called brethren and nothing higher. Therefore Paul sanctioned their request and laid down a code of conduct for bishops.

> This is a true saying, if a man desire the office of a bishop, he desireth a good work. A bishop then must be blameless, the husband of one wife, vigilant, sober, of good behaviour, given to hospitality, apt to teach; Not given to wine, no striker, not greedy of filthy lucre; but patient, not a brawler, not covetous; One that ruleth well his own house, having his children in subjection with all gravity; (For if a man know not how to rule his own house, how shall he take care of the church of God?) Not a novice, lest being lifted up with

> pride he fall into the condemnation of the devil. Moreover he must have a good report of them which are without; lest he fall into reproach and the snare of the devil. Likewise must the deacons be grave, not doubletongued, not given to much wine, not greedy of filthy lucre; Holding the mystery of the faith in a pure conscience. And let these also first be proved; then let them use the office of a deacon, being found blameless. Even so must their wives be grave, not slanderers, sober, faithful in all things. (1 Timothy 3:1–11)

Let us face reality here: Jesus came all the way from the first heaven to earth and laid down His command. Who then can change it? Let us abide in the Lord's command, as Jesus said to His disciples in Matthew 23:8 and 11 "But be not ye called Rabbi: for one is your Master, even Christ; and all ye are brethren … But he that is greatest among you shall be your servant."

Kings, presidents, prime ministers, lawyers, and politicians: All of these authorities are of the world and have no jurisdiction with God. (Here I speak of the office, not the individual; if the individual believes that Jesus is the Son of God, he or she is saved, but he or she must give up the office to be drawn unto Jesus.) When Jesus was upon earth, the Jews who did not believe that He was the Son of God, tried to condemn Him by asking Him a question: Is it right to pay taxes unto Caesar? Let us go into the Scriptures to see what Jesus said in reply.

> Then went the Pharisees, and took counsel how they might entangle him in his talk. And they sent out unto him their disciples with the Herodians, saying, Master, we know that thou art true, and teachest the way of God in truth, neither carest thou for any man: for thou regardest not the person of men. Tell us therefore, what thinkest thou? Is it lawful to give tribute unto Caesar, or not? But Jesus perceived their wickedness, and said, why tempt ye me, ye hypocrites? Shew me the tribute money. And they brought unto him a penny. And he saith unto them, whose is this image and superscription? They say unto him, Caesar's. Then saith he unto them, Render therefore unto Caesar the things which are Caesar's; and unto God the things that are God's. When they had heard these words, they marvelled, and left him, and went their way. (Matthew 22:15–22)

This tells us that we cannot serve the authorities and God at the same time; one must be neglected. Therefore the one that is not present by sight and has only given a promise is the one that is most likely to be neglected. I want you to know that the promise of eternal Life from God is for all of us who do the will of the Father; however, we must give up fame, fortune, riches, and power to receive it. Will you give up all power and riches for a seat at the heavenly Father's table to eat of the Tree of Life so you will live forever? Let us look at the following Scriptures.

John 3:16 says, "For God so loved the world, that he gave his only begotten Son, that whosoever believeth in him should not perish, but have everlasting life."

Anyone who believes is saved; it does not matter what his or her position is in life. But there is a next save that calls for action. Give up luxuries in life and pray that the Father will draw you unto His Son. Matthew 19:29 says, "And every one that hath forsaken houses, or brethren, or sisters, or father, or mother, or wife, or children, or lands, for my name's sake, shall receive a hundredfold, and shall inherit everlasting life." Jesus sent His servant Ananias to pray for Saul/Paul that he would receive his sight and take His message to the Gentiles, kings, and Jews. Paul was a highly respected Jew. He walked among kings and was a citizen of Rome. He gave up everything. Even though he was compelled, he is an example that shows we must give up our worldly possessions. Acts 9:15 says, "But the Lord said unto him, Go thy way: for he is a chosen vessel unto me, to bear my name before the Gentiles, and kings, and the children of Israel." It is hard for a person with high position and big salary and who is well respected by others to give it all up and serve God. Many politicians are lawyers. Here is what Jesus said to lawyers:

> Then answered one of the lawyers, and said unto him, Master, thus saying thou reproachest us also. and he said, Woe unto you also, ye lawyers! For ye lade men with burdens grievous to be borne, and ye yourselves touch not the burdens with one of your fingers … Woe unto you, lawyers! For ye have taken away the key of knowledge: ye entered

> not in yourselves, and them that were entering in ye hindered. (Luke 11:45–46 and 52)

Do you know of any lawyer who will give up his practice and title for the gospel of God? I don't. It would be very few, if any. Giving it all up must be done from the heart, by faith not by fate. We should have no thought of seeking a reward here on earth. The Father, who sees our hearts, will reward us when Jesus returns as said in Matthew 16:27: "For the Son of man shall come in the glory of his Father with his angels; and then he shall reward every man according to his works." [Reward every man means all that the Father has drawn unto the Son, the others, Jesus will send into outer darkness].

Let us understand that anyone who believes that Jesus is the Son of God is saved. It does not matter if you are a king, pope, priest, bishop, false prophet; pastor, president, prime minister, lawyer or politician; once you believe, and then you are saved. John 1:12 says, "But as many as received him, to them gave he power to become the sons of God, even to them that believe on his name." When you leave this earth, you will no doubt go to the third heaven/paradise and tarry there until Jesus returns. Here is what Jesus said to Peter about Judas, who was following Jesus on His way to be ascended. (We know it was Judas because Jesus loved him. He trusted him with the money and brought him up from the grave when He arose in Matthew 27:52). It was not John because Peter was in no position to question John following Jesus.

> Then Peter, turning about, seeth the disciple whom Jesus loved following; which also leaned

> on his breast at supper, and said, Lord, which is he that betrayeth thee? Peter seeing him saith to Jesus, Lord, and what shall this man do? Jesus saith unto him, if I will that he tarry till I come, what is that to thee? Follow thou me. (John 21:20–22)

We understand that Judas, who also believed, was taken to paradise to tarry until Jesus returns, just as all other believers. However, while we are here on earth, if we do not heed the words of the Lord Jesus and get rid of fame and riches, then we ask the greatest religious question: Will Jesus put us on His right hand when He return and take us with Him to the Father's heaven? Here is a question Jesus asked the Jews, Luke 6:46 says, "And why call ye me, Lord, Lord, and do not the things which I say?" Many will not go with Jesus when He returns because they have not pleased the Father. To please the Father, we must let our light shine. We must come out of the building and go into the field and get rid of the big names and fortunes. You cannot worship the Father in a building, and He is seeking those who will worship Him. Let us look at the following Scriptures:

> For many are called, but few are chosen. (Matthew 22:14)

> But the hour cometh and now is, when the true worshippers shall worship the Father in spirit and in truth: for the Father seeketh such to worship him. (John 4:23)

Let your light so shine before men, that they may see your good works, and glorify your Father which is in heaven. (Matthew 5:16).

No man can come to me, except the Father which hath sent me draw him: and I will raise him up at the last day. (John 6:44)

And a certain ruler asked him, saying, Good Master, what shall I do to inherit eternal life? And Jesus said unto him, Why callest thou me good? None is good, save one, that is, God. Thou knowest the commandments, do not commit adultery, do not kill, Do not steal, Do not bear false witness, Honour thy father and thy mother. And he said, All these have I kept from my youth up. Now when Jesus heard these things, he said unto him, Yet lackest thou one thing: sell all that thou hast, and distribute unto the poor, and thou shalt have treasure in heaven: and come, follow me. And when he heard this, he was very sorrowful: for he was very rich. And when Jesus saw that he was very sorrowful, he said, how hardly shall they that have riches enter into the kingdom of God! For it is easier for a camel to go through a needle's eye, than for a rich man to enter into the kingdom of God. (Luke 18:18–25)

I want to make it clear and simple: when we believe that Jesus is the Son of God, we are saved, which is the first save. It does not matter who or what we are in life—rich or poor, powerful or powerless. Jesus said that whosoever lives and believes in Him shall never die. John said that as many as received Him, to them He gave power to become the sons of God, even to those who believe on His name. The dying man on the cross believed, and he was saved. There was once a convicted serial killer on his way to be put to death when he said that he gave his life to Christ; he also is saved in the first save. All who believe are saved from death and will not suffer pain and agony; they will fall into a deep sleep, as understood in the book of Luke. There was a ruler of the synagogue named Jairus whose twelve-year-old daughter was sick. He went for Jesus to come to his house to heal his daughter. While he waited for the Master, one of his servants told him that his daughter had died. Let us read what happened when Jesus told the people that she was only asleep.

> But when Jesus heard it, he answered him, saying, Fear not: believe only, and she shall be made whole. And when he came into the house, he suffered no man to go in, save Peter, and James, and John, and the father and the mother of the maiden. And all wept, and bewailed her: but he said, Weep not; she is not dead, but sleepeth. And they laughed him to scorn, knowing that she was dead. And he put them all out, and took her by the hand, and called, saying, Maid, arise. And her

> spirit came again, and she arose straightway: and
> he commanded to give her meat. (Luke 8:50–55)

All who believe will sleep-go to rest in paradise-third heaven; only the Father can second save us from damnation, as we understand in John 6:44, we must please the Father while here on earth by obeying the words of the Lord Jesus that the Father will draw us unto the Son before we leave this earth, not this world, remember the third heaven/paradise is between the sea and clouds where the birds fly. Jesus took the saved man on the cross there, and He will set up his throne there Matthew 25:31 when He returns from the Father's kingdom-first heaven. There is also a paradise in the first heaven (Revelation 2:7). No man on earth has ever gone there; only Jesus who came down and went back up knows its location.

Now as I conclude this sermon, let us go through a process of understanding. We know that the Father Himself brought His Son Jesus down to earth through the virgin Mary, as it says in Luke 1:35: "And the angel answered and said unto her, The Holy Ghost shall come upon thee, and the power of the Highest shall overshadow thee: therefore also that holy thing which shall be born of thee shall be called the Son of God." We know that Jesus is the Christ and the Messiah, as it says in John 4:25–26: "The woman saith unto him, I know that Messias cometh, which is called Christ: when he is come, he will tell us all things. Jesus saith unto her, I that speak unto thee am he." We know that Jesus was sent to the Jews, not the Gentiles, as it says in Matthew 15:24: "But he answered and said, I am not sent but unto the lost sheep of the house of Israel." We know that He was anointed to preach the gospel to the poor, as it says in Luke 4:18: "The Spirit of the Lord is upon me, because he hath anointed me to preach the gospel to the poor; he hath sent me to heal the brokenhearted, to preach deliverance to the captives, and recovering of sight to the blind, to set at liberty them that are bruised."

We know that the Jews did not receive Him, as it says in John 1:11: "He came unto his own, and his own received him not." We know that the present-day Jews are condemned, as it says in Luke 14:24: "For I say unto you, that none of those men which were bidden shall taste of my supper." We know that Jesus sent an invitation with Paul to the Gentiles, as it says in Luke 14:23: "And the lord said unto the servant, Go out into the highways and hedges, and compel them to come in, that my house may be filled." Acts 9:15 says, "But the Lord said unto him, go thy way: for he is a chosen vessel unto me, to bear my name before the Gentiles, and kings, and the children of Israel." We know that should we have a higher authority/position than Jesus; the Father will not draw us unto His Son.

> But be not ye called Rabbi: for one is your Master, even Christ; and all ye are brethren. And call no man your father upon the earth: for one is your Father, which is in heaven. Neither be ye called masters: for one is your Master, even Christ. But he that is greatest among you shall be your servant. And whosoever shall exalt himself shall be abased; and he that shall humble himself shall be exalted. (Matthew 32:8–12)

We know that anyone who harms a little child will not be drawn unto Jesus:

> But whoso shall offend one of these little ones which believe in me, it were better for him that a millstone were hanged about his neck, and that he were drowned in the depth of the sea … Take heed that ye despise not one of these little ones; for I say unto you, that in heaven their angels do always behold the face of my Father which is in heaven. (Matthew 18:6, 10)

Finally we know that we should not partake of the ungodly things of this world, more particularly, having more than one living wife or husband and having sex out of marriage, as the Lord Jesus said it would happen.

> But as the days of Noah were, so shall also the coming of the Son of man be. For as in the days that were before the flood they were eating and drinking, marrying and giving in marriage, until the day that Noe entered into the ark. (Matthew 24:37–38)

I cannot emphasize this enough: Jesus cannot take us to the Father if the Father does not convert/draw us unto Jesus. John 6:65 says, "And he said, therefore said I unto you, that no man can come unto me, except it were given unto him of my Father." I also want us to be absolutely clear on this—beginning from

Adam up to you, there is no man ever on this earth who has gone to the Father's kingdom except Jesus, and only He can take us there. John 3:13 says, "And no man hath ascended up to heaven, but he that came down from heaven, even the Son of man which is in heaven."

We must decide now before it is too late. Many in the third heaven would like to come back and live a different life. However, it is too late for them; will you also wait until it is too late? Get rid of those riches, big names, and authority; serve the Lord in spirit and in truth so He may draw you unto His Son that He will put you on His right hand as sheep and not on His left hand as goats.

> When the Son of man shall come in his glory, and all the holy angels with him, then shall he sit upon the throne of his glory: And before him shall be gathered all nations: and he shall separate them one from another, as a shepherd divideth his sheep from the goats: And he shall set the sheep on his right hand, but the goats on the left. Then shall the King say unto them on his right hand, Come, ye blessed of my Father, inherit the kingdom prepared for you from the foundation of the world. (Matthew 25:31–34)

And this, my brothers and sisters, is the greatest religious question: Will Jesus put you on His right hand as sheep or on His left hand as goats? It is your decision. God bless you.

(4)

Why Did Jesus (God) Come to Earth in the Flesh?

Before I go into the message, I will give you an understanding of the saints. Where are they, now and where were they before Jesus came to earth?

Please note here that all Saints are believers but not all believers are saints. Saints, also referred to as sheep are people God the Father has chosen to wait (sleep, rest, or tarry) in the third heaven for Jesus' return to take them to the Father's kingdom. The same as it was with Noah; the earth will be destroyed and re-beautified that the saints may happily dwell upon it.

Where Were the Saints/Sheep before Jesus Arose from the Grave?

In Luke 16:22 Jesus spoke about a rich man who died and was buried. He opened his eyes in torment, but a poor man was carried off by angels into Abraham's bosom. This is where the saints were. Jesus referred to them as other sheep. John 10:16 says,

"And other sheep I have, which are not of this fold: them also I must bring, and they shall hear my voice; and there shall be one fold, and one shepherd." John 11:25 says, "Jesus said unto her, I am the resurrection, and the life: he that believeth in me, though he were dead, yet shall he live." We see in Matthew 27:52 that Jesus brought the saints up so they would live and hear His voice. Judas, who killed himself, also came up because he believed. They were all taken to third heaven/paradise to tarry until Jesus' return.

Why Did Jesus Come to Earth in the Flesh?

I will be speaking on three reasons why Jesus came to earth: (1) to invite the Jews; (2) to redeem mankind to the Father; and (3) to assess the fleshly problems that humans encounter so they may be eliminated from the new earth.

(1) We understand that the Jews are God's chosen people who worshipped Him, and all other people are Gentiles, who had worshipped other gods. The Jews were in and out of favor with God until He told them that He would not pass by them anymore (Amos 7:8, 8:2). God continued to love the Jews. He sent His only begotten Son, Jesus the Christ, to them (Matthew 15:24). He invited them to His kingdom (the first heaven) to wait until He completes the new earth. The Jews rejected the invite and ordered God's Son to death, and the Gentiles crucified him.

(2) The Father then extended His invitation to the Gentiles, and as Jesus said in John 11:26 that all who believe that He is who the Father said that He is (Matthew 3:17 and

17:5), His beloved Son. Once you believe, you will not die. You are saved from death. You have saved yourself by heeding Jesus' call to believe. You can also turn back by converting to some other belief (Luke 9:62) that Jesus is not the Son of God. If you only believe, it qualifies you to go into the paradise/third heaven (Luke 23:43). The believed thief on the cross went there and many false prophets are there because they believe. Many people believe, but they do not have the love of God in their hearts. They see others in need and do not care to help them. They are always looking for what they can get and do not care to give. Jesus wants us to tell others of His words as found in the four gospels, Matthew, Mark, Luke, and John. He is telling us what we must do. Jesus said in Luke 6:46, "And why call ye me, Lord, Lord, and do not the things which I say?" And He said in John 6:63, "It is the spirit that quickeneth; the flesh profiteth nothing: the words that I speak unto you, they are spirit, and they are life." Matthew 5:16 says, "Let your light so shine before men, that they may see your good works, and glorify your Father which is in heaven." We have to do more than just believe because the Father is seeking true worshippers.

John 4:23 says, "But the hour cometh, and now is, when the true worshippers shall worship the Father in spirit and in truth: for the Father seeketh such to worship him." Many are called but few are chosen (Matthew 22:14). Only the Father can choose who He wants to come into His kingdom, which is the first heaven.

Only He can second save you from damnation. Many in paradise will not go with Jesus to the Father. It is our responsibility to do the works of the Father so He may draw us unto His Son, as we see in Matthew 7:21–23.

> Not everyone that saith unto me, Lord, Lord, shall enter into the kingdom of heaven; but he that doeth the will of my Father which is in heaven. Many will say to me in that day, Lord, Lord, have we not prophesied in thy name? And in thy name have cast out devils? And in thy name done many wonderful works? And then will I profess unto them, I never knew you: depart from me, ye that work iniquity.

Jesus will say that to people with higher names than brethren because He said that all names above brethren belong to Him, and if you lift yourself up, He will bring you down and the Father will not draw you unto Him. The next Scripture is speaking to all those vain worshippers in the building unlawfully called the church (Matthew 6:5), who refuse to come out of the building and go into the field and explain the three heavens and two saves to all who would listen, so the Father may draw them unto His Son. Therefore the Son will take them to the Father.

> And I say unto you, That many shall come from the east and west, and shall sit down with Abraham, and Isaac, and Jacob, in the kingdom of heaven. But the children of the kingdom shall be cast out

> into outer darkness: there shall be weeping and gnashing of teeth. (Matthew 8:11–12)

This will be a sad moment. Why? Because many are saved from death and are contented here on earth, but because they have not pleased the Father, they are not drawn unto the Son (not second saved). Therefore Jesus cannot take them with Him to the Father. Jesus said go to the Father in Jesus' name. John 14:6 says, "Jesus saith unto him, I am the way, the truth, and the life: no man cometh unto the Father, but by me." (This means you must pray to the Father in Jesus' name, and only Jesus can take you to the Father.) Ask the Father to draw you unto His Son, Jesus. John 6:44 says, "No man can come to me, except the Father which hath sent me draw him: and I will raise him up at the last day." Let your light shine (Matthew 5:16) so the Father may be glorified through your good works.

When the Father draws you, second saves you, converts you as Jesus prayed the Father to convert Peter (Luke 22:32), no one can unsaved you. There can be no looking back or backsliding (John 10:28). There is absolutely nothing anyone inside the building called church can do to second save you. You were first saved before you went into the building/church. Come out of the padded pews, and go into the fields. As you pray that the Lord will use you, pray also that the Lord of the harvest will send forth laborers into the harvest. Jesus said that the harvest is plenteous but the laborers are few. He sent His disciples out and He is asking us to go out, but most of us want to hang out in air-conditioning and satisfy men. Let us go into the highways and hedges where the Father is telling us to go (Luke 14:23). Matthew 10:32 says,

"Whosoever therefore shall confess me before men, him will I confess also before my Father which is in heaven."

Women of God out in the field, dress not provocatively. Let us remember we are only invited guests to God's kingdom. If we know that almighty God does not like something (Deuteronomy 22:5), we should not do it. Let your desire be unto your one living husband, as God has commanded in Genesis 3:16: "Unto the woman he said, I will greatly multiply thy sorrow and thy conception; in sorrow thou shalt bring forth children; and thy desire shall be to thy husband, and he shall rule over thee." If you do not have a husband, be celibate and remain to yourself, if you really love God.

(3) Jesus came to earth in the flesh to see why is it so hard for man to worship the Father in spirit and in truth and to show us the easiest way to serve the Father now in these worst conditions, with Satan doing his utmost to keep us from God. We must keep in mind these examples set by Jesus, be humble and not proud, with no big titles. We must not be rich. We should show God's love one toward another and always give freely. If we follow these examples, we will not find it hard to worship the Father in spirit and in truth.

Jesus also came to earth in the flesh to seek out the hard and unnecessary things that mankind has to bear so they will be eliminated from the new earth. I think the biggest complaint Jesus got from man is man's relationship with woman. Jesus said if you look with lust at a woman, you commit adultery already in your heart (Matthew 5:28). Take a look at some of the things that will be eliminated from the Holy City.

We see in Matthew 22:30 Jesus said there will be no more husband and wife. In Revelation 20:10 there will be no more temptations. Satan, the Devil, will be gone. In Revelation 21:1 there will be no more sea. In Revelation 21:4 there will be no more death, crying, sickness, sorrows, or pain. And Revelation 21:23 says there will be no more sun because Jesus, God's Son, will be the light.

As I end this sermon, I wish to remind you that Jesus said in Luke 16:16 the Law and the prophets were until John (the Baptist). That means there will be no more laws and no more prophets to come to the Jews. (No Law or prophets were ever sent to the Gentiles.) Jesus is saying that any law or prophet that comes after John is false. We must shun them. Some time ago, I was asked to explain Luke 5:37, which is about new wine in old bottles. As the Spirit gave me the understanding, so give I unto you. What Jesus was saying is that John preached the Law and Jesus preached the kingdom of God. Should you put the kingdom of God in the law, then the Law is overpowered by the kingdom of God. Let us understand that the Father will not send any law with any prophet to the Jews after they rejected His Son. A matter of fact, no unconverted Jew will enter the kingdom of God. Matthew 22:8 says, "Then saith he to his servants, the wedding is ready, but they which were bidden were not worthy."

That means the Jews are not worthy. What can they do? Believe that Jesus is the Son of God. Remember that salvation came not by the law, but through Jesus Christ are we saved.

Let's pray. Our Father in heaven, we give You thanks for Your Word and all who would heed it that You will draw them unto Your Son so they may do a work in Your harvest and that we may be ready to go with Jesus when He returns (Matthew 25:31–34). We pray in Jesus' name. Amen.

God bless you.

(5)

A Mysterious Woman of the Bible

I am compelled to write to you about this woman and the glory of what she has done. We see in the Holy Bible (King James Version) in Matthew 26:13 and Mark 14:9 that Jesus commanded what she did must be preached around the world. Let us take a look at what Jesus said in Matthew 26:13: "Verily I say unto you, wheresoever this gospel shall be preached in the whole world, there shall also this, that this woman hath done, be told for a memorial of her." Now here is a woman about who very little is known, not even her name; that may be the reason why she is not often preached about. The little she did for Jesus (anointed His body for burial) was more than anyone else was able to do (save Mary, His mother). We see that Mary Magdalene and other women went to anoint Jesus' body on the resurrection day after the Sabbath. Mark 16:1 says, "And when the Sabbath was past, Mary Magdalene, and Mary the mother of James, and Salome, had bought sweet spices, that they might come and anoint him." Only to their surprise, they found the tomb empty.

While Jesus was in Bethany, less than a week before the Last Super, He was invited to a dinner by a Pharisee called Simon the Leper. Luke 7:36 says, "And one of the Pharisees desired him that he would eat with him. And he went into the Pharisee's house, and sat down to meat." A mysterious woman went in to Jesus. She was known to the high priest and men of God as a sinner (an outcast), not fit even to touch them.

> Now when the Pharisee which had bidden him saw it, he spake within himself, saying, This man, if he were a prophet, would have known who and what manner of woman this is that toucheth him: for she is a sinner. And Jesus answering said unto him, Simon, I have somewhat to say unto thee. And he saith, Master, say on. (Luke 7:39–40)

We understand from that passage of Scripture that Simon the leper had evil thoughts in his heart. Jesus knew his thoughts and stopped him before he was able to put the uninvited woman out. I believe that Simon the leper, as he is called in Matthew 26:6–7, may have had a healing encounter with Jesus since he is known as the leper. The Jews at that time deemed lepers unclean, and they could not mix with normal people until they were certified cured by a priest. We want to note here that it is recorded in both Matthew and Mark where the unnamed woman poured ointment on Jesus' head and body, and He was in Bethany at Simon's house, not the house of Mary, Martha, and Lazarus, which was also in Bethany, where they hosted a dinner for Jesus days earlier in John 11:1–2: "Now a certain man was sick, named Lazarus, of Bethany, the town of Mary and her sister Martha. (It was that Mary which anointed the Lord with ointment, and wiped his feet with her hair, whose brother Lazarus was sick.)" What we understand from this Scripture is that Mary, who was not a sinner, did not weep on Jesus' feet.

> Then Jesus six days before the Passover came to Bethany, where Lazarus was, which had been dead, whom he raised from the dead. There they made him a supper; and Martha served: but Lazarus was one of them that sat at the table with him. Then took Mary a pound of ointment of spikenard, very costly, and anointed the feet of Jesus, and wiped his feet with her hair: and the house was filled with the odor of the ointment. (John 12:1–3)

Remember, Mary did not wash Jesus' feet with tears. Jesus spent three days in Bethany:

> And he went through the cities and villages, teaching, and journeying toward Jerusalem … Nevertheless I must walk to day, and to-morrow, and the day following: for it cannot be that a prophet perishes out of Jerusalem. (Luke 13:22 and 33)

We don't know very much about this mysterious woman. Let us read what is said about her in Luke 7:37–38.

> And, behold, a woman in the city, which was a sinner, when she knew that Jesus sat at meat in the Pharisee's house, brought an alabaster box of ointment. And stood at his feet behind him weeping, and began to wash his feet with tears, and did wipe them with the hairs of her head, and kissed his feet, and anointed them with the ointment.

We understand that the woman was in the city, no doubt doing business. Was she rich or poor? Did she have the expensive ointment with her, or did she go home and get it? Maybe she bought it. Gentiles were also known as sinners. Was she a Jew or Gentile? Whatever the mystery, she was bold enough to enter the home of a leader of the Jews uninvited. This woman prepared Jesus' body for burial by pouring the precious ointment over His body from head to toe, washed his feet with her tears, dried them with her hair, and anointed and continually kissed His feet. Who was this woman? Mary the sister of Lazarus also did some anointing; Jesus gave an account for her ointment, as we see in John 12:7: "Then said Jesus, Let her alone: against the day of my burying hath she kept this." Mary was at home when she got the ointment, not at the Pharisee's house. The Scripture said that Mary had a pound of ointment. Whether it was in an alabaster box we don't know, but we do know that the woman of the city had an alabaster box. Therefore I will call the sinner woman "the alabaster lady," as she is often known. There is no mention in the Scriptures as to who this mysterious woman really is. However, we are to remember her works. Some people called her Mary, the sister of Lazarus; some say she is Mary Magdalene of Magdala; and others refer to her as the woman caught in the act of adultery, which was taken to Jesus to see what He would do with her. Let us take a look at all of these women to see why they cannot be the mysterious woman.

(1) Mary the sister of Lazarus who anointed Jesus' feet seven days before His burial at their home in Bethany, where they made a supper for Him. She cannot be the mysterious woman because she did not have many sins. The Scriptures do not say that she anointed Jesus' head and body, and neither did she weep and wash his feet with her tears. In all fairness to Mary, John 11:2 says, "(It was that Mary which anointed the Lord with ointment, and wiped his feet with her hair, whose brother Lazarus was sick.)" John said that she anointed the Lord and Jesus said that "against the day of his burying hath she kept the ointment." There is no mention of anointing His head and body or of crying on His feet. However we know that Mary and her family were loved and well known by the society. Had it been her, they would have said it was Mary, as we read earlier in John 12:3. Therefore we rule out Mary the sister of Lazarus.

(2) Mary Magdalene of Magdala of Galilee, out of whom seven devils were cast, is sometimes identified as this mysterious woman. Luke 8:2 says, "And certain women, which had been healed of evil spirits and infirmities, Mary called Magdalene, out of whom went seven devils." It could not have been her. After Jesus healed her, she

followed and served Him. Mark 15:40–41 says, "There were also women looking on afar off: among whom was Mary Magdalene, and Mary the mother of James the less and of Joses, and Salome (Who also, when he was in Galilee, followed him, and ministered unto him) and many other women which came up with him unto Jerusalem." We see that even at the resurrection Mary Magdalene was there. Mark 16:9 says, "Now when Jesus was risen early the first day of the week, he appeared first to Mary Magdalene, out of whom he had cast seven devils." Therefore we know that Mary Magdalene could not have been the mysterious woman because her sins were already forgiven and she was also well known. Therefore we rule her out.

(3) The woman caught in the act of adultery that was taken to Jesus by the Scribes and Pharisees that they might test Him is sometimes identified as the mysterious. She could not have been the mysterious woman because her sins had already been forgiven, and she was told to go and sin no more. John 8:11 says, "She said, No man, Lord. And Jesus said unto her, neither do I condemn thee: go, and sin no more." Therefore we also rule her out.

A note of interest: Jesus and His disciple Judas, the betrayer son of Simon, were both born in Judaea; Jesus' other disciples were all from Galilee, where Jesus grew up. Now let us look at John 12:4: "Then saith one of his disciples, Judas Iscariot, Simon's son, which should betray him." Is this Simon the father of Judas also the Pharisee who invited Jesus to dinner? Luke 7:36, 40 says, "And one of the Pharisees desired him that he would eat with him. And he went into the Pharisee's house, and sat down to meat ... And Jesus answering said unto him, Simon, I have somewhat to say unto thee. And he saith, Master, say on."

Conclusion

There are no less than seven Simons mention in the Bible (KJV). Let us look at them.

(1) Simon Peter in Matthew 10:2
(2) Simon the Canaanite in Matthew 10:4, also called the Zelotes in Luke 6:15
(3) Simon the leper in Matthew 26:6
(4) Simon of Cyrene in Matthew 27:32
(5) Simon, father of Judas Iscariot, in John 6:71
(6) Simon the sorcerer in Acts 8:9
(7) Simon the tanner in Acts 9:43

There are two mention of Jesus being anointed, both in Bethany, a three-day walk to Jerusalem. Luke 13:33 says, "Nevertheless I must walk to day, and tomorrow, and the day following: for it cannot be that a prophet perish out of Jerusalem."

The first anointing was at Lazarus' house six days before Passover (John 12:1). He was anointed by Mary, sister of Martha and Lazarus. She used a pound of ointment of spikenard, which was very costly.

The second anointing was at the house of Simon the leper, a Pharisee, three days before Passover (Luke 13:33). He was anointed by an unnamed mysterious woman who was a sinner. She used an alabaster box of ointment of spikenard, which was very precious.

This alabaster lady's heart was full of repentance, and the Father sent her unto His Son, where she labored for the Master, and now she was free indeed. Jesus wants us to preach about her action so she may long be remembered. We have learned from this that the Father draws us unto His Son, Jesus. John 6:44 says, "No man can come to me, except the Father which hath sent me draw him: and I will raise him up at the last day." We must be obedient unto the Holy Spirit. John 16:13 says, "Howbeit when he, the Spirit of truth, is come, he will guide you into all truth: for he shall not speak of himself; but whatsoever he shall hear, that shall he speak: and he will shew you things to come."

We must let the Holy Spirit lead us. Sometimes we have to be bold, as was the alabaster lady. She went into the Pharisee's home uninvited, even into the dining room. She really was bold. Even though her name is a mystery unto us, we will know her in the third heaven when we get there. I wonder if she knew she was preparing the Lord's body for burial; her weeping could have been because she knew He was going to die. She also could have been weeping because of remorse for her many sins. Whatever the reason, she was prepared to withstand the consequence even if it cost her life, as Esther said in Esther 4:16: "Go, gather together all the Jews that are present in Shushan, and fast ye for me, and neither eat nor drink three days, night or day: I also and my maidens will fast likewise; and so will I go in unto the king, which is not according to the law: and if I perish, I perish."

God bless you.

(6)

A Closer Look at Two Saves

My brothers and sisters in the Lord, it is my prayer that you understand this message and tell others about it that they too may understand the two saves before it is too late.

All of the Scriptures are taken from the Holy Bible (KJV) and are easy for you to read. The first save is when you believe that Jesus Christ is the Messiah and the Son of God and are saved from death (John 1:11–12, John 3:16–17, John 11:25–26). Even your children up to age twelve believe because you believe (Matthew 18:6, 10). If you do not believe you will die, when you leave this earth, and go to a place of torment called hell (John 3:18, Luke 16: 23).

The Father first sent His Son, Jesus, to the Jews to invite them to His kingdom (Matthew 22:3, 10:6, 15:24) That He would destroy and renew the Earth again as with Noah and the Flood" (Matthew 24:39). The righteous Jews did not receive Jesus. Only some outcast Jews believed (Luke 15:1–2, 31–32, 13:23–24, 34). Jesus first invited the Gentiles to the Father's house by sending the Holy Ghost upon them (Acts 2:7–8, 37–38, 41, Luke 14:21–22).

The Father then told Jesus to compel the Gentiles to come into His house (Luke 14:23). Jesus then compelled Saul, later known as Paul, to invite the Gentiles (Acts 9:3–6, 15–16). Paul's message to us is to first believe and second be baptized by the Holy Ghost, controlled by the heavenly Father (not by water, which is John's baptism) (Matthew 3:11, Acts 19:1–7). Only the Father God baptizes and converts us (Matthew 13:15, 18:3, Luke 22:31–32). Here we see Peter, who walked on water, was saved from death but not baptized with the Holy Ghost, not converted. Now we will look at the second save.

The second save is when we are saved from damnation and do the will of the Father so He will draw us unto the Son (John 14:21, 6:44). Jesus said that if we believe, we will not die but will go into the third heaven-paradise (Luke 23:43, 2 Corinthians 12:2–4) and tarry there till He returns (John 21:22). Before we leave this earth, we must do the will of the Father so He will draw us onto the Son. These Scriptures tell us some things the Father wants us to do: Matthew 5:16, 7:12, 21, Mark 12:30–31, Luke 16:13, and John 14:21. If we do not do these things and the Father does not draw us onto His Son, when Jesus returns and sets up His throne in the third heaven-paradise (Matthew 25:31–34), He will put those who don't do His will (James 1:22) on His left as goats, and they will die (Matthew 16:28). All who did the will of the Father and who He has drawn unto the Son will go on the right as sheep. Jesus will take these people back with Him to the Father. That is the second save.

We must explain the two saves (saved from death and saved from damnation) to our love ones; do not wait until they are gone, that is too late. There are some that tells us to go and make disciples of men. This is wrong (Matthew 28:19) Jesus said we should teach all nations. Only God makes disciples (John 6:45, 65, John 17:6).

There are many who have gone on to rest until Jesus return, and they now realized that they did not do the will of the Father and He did not draw them unto His Son—but it is too late. There is nothing they can do. Here are two Scriptures that will lead us to that understanding. The rich man in hell wanted Abraham to send the poor man back to earth to tell his brothers to live right in Luke 16:27–28: "Then he said, I pray thee therefore, father, that thou wouldest send him to my father's house: For I have five brethren; that he may testify unto them, lest they also come into this place of torment." Then a man who was in third heaven-paradise told Paul of the turmoil in paradise-heaven. People want to come back to earth to live right or send message to their loved ones that they do the will of God, but it is too late, they cannot live their lives over again and they cannot warn anyone of the wrath to come; John and Jesus already done that (Matthew 3:7 and John 3:36). Here is what Paul said;

> I knew a man in Christ above fourteen years ago, (whether in the body, I cannot tell; or whether out of the body, I cannot tell: God knoweth;) such an one caught up to the third heaven. And I knew such a man, (whether in the body, or out of the body, I cannot tell: God knoweth;) How that he was caught up into paradise, and heard unspeakable words, which it is not lawful for a man to utter. (2 Corinthians 12:2–4)

Even though the believers in heaven want to tell us to live right and do God's will, they are not able to. Let us heed the words of the Lord Jesus in Matthew 5:16: "Let your light so shine before men, that they may see your good works, and glorify your Father which is in heaven." Now that you have the understanding, never stop telling others about the two saves. Where possible read this book aloud to your family especially your kids, make it fun, let them help with finding the scriptures and compliment them even if you find it first. (Proverbs 22:6).

God bless you.

(7)

Can The Rich Enter Heaven? (Hardly)

Before we look at what the Bible says about the topic, let me relate to you some of my experiences of trying to become rich. I am in my mid-sixties, and ever since I knew about wealth, I have desired to be rich. I had numerous of opportunities to become rich until in my late-fifties, when the Holy Spirit made me understand that I am not to rich. Because of space, I will only tell you about three of my experiences.

First, in my early working years while I was working on a cruise ship between Nassau and Miami, I met a rich car dealer in Miami who told me that he would ship all the vehicles I needed on consignment to Nassau for me to start a car sales. All I needed was to find the lot. At that time, property was cheap. Why it did not materialize? I don't know.

Second, after our retirement from our thirty-year career, my wife and I moved to Florida, where we played the lotto frequently until the Holy Spirit told me to stop. About four years before I was told to stop, I saw a website on the computer that asked me to enter my numbers to see if they had ever come in. After I checked my numbers and none of them were ever played, I checked my wife's numbers, and two of them showed up, with less than thirty days between each other. I jumped up from the computer shouting, "We are rich!" At that time my wife had played the same numbers for about two years, and she got so disappointed with not winning that she just put her tickets away to check them later. We checked all her tickets, only to find she did not buy any on those two dates. Why not?

My last attempt to become rich was in my mid-fifties. I entered a Florida court auction to buy and sell homes. I won the bid on a half-duplex for thirty five thousand dollars, the value of which was two hundred and thirty thousand dollars. The auction sale was in two parts. I had a confirmed loan at the bank to bid on the second part, which was the main mortgage for the half duplex. The first part was a lien. However, when I went to the bank for the loan, I was told that the banks had stopped lending because the housing market had crashed. The second bid went higher than the cash I had; therefore I lost the thirty five thousand dollars. I had intended to continue the auction and make my money back. Now that I understand the Word of God, I know not to strive for riches. I quit pursuing riches.

I am so glad that our Father in heaven tells of His love in the book He has given us. Let us now go into the King James Version of the Holy Bible and see what it says about rich men. Here we see a rich man who went to Jesus seeking eternal life, but he did not want to give up his riches.

> Jesus said unto him, if thou wilt be perfect, go and sell that thou hast, and give to the poor, and

> thou shalt have treasure in heaven: and come and follow me … Then said Jesus unto his disciples, Verily I say unto you, that a rich man shall hardly enter into the kingdom of heaven. And again I say unto you, it's easier for a camel to go through the eye of a needle, than for a rich man to enter into the kingdom of God. (Matthew 19:21, 23–24, emphasis added)

As Christians, if we give to the poor when God gives to us and lay up not treasures on earth, we will never be rich. Note, Jesus said "eye of a needle" which is not the gate called the Needle's Eye**.** Jesus taught us this in Matthew 6:19, 21, and 24.

> Lay not up for yourselves treasures upon earth, where moth and rust doth corrupt, and where thieves break through and steal … For where your treasure is, there will your heart be also … No man can serve two masters: for either he will hate the one, and love the other; or else he will hold to the one, and despise the other. Ye cannot serve God and mammon.

Hear what Jesus said in the parable of the sower about riches Luke 8:14: "And that which fell among thorns are they, which, when they have heard, go forth, and are choked with cares and riches and pleasures of this life, and bring no fruit to perfection." Jesus was anointed to preach the gospel to the poor as seen in Luke 4:18: "The Spirit of the Lord is upon me, because he hath anointed me to preach the gospel to the poor; he hath sent me to heal the brokenhearted, to preach deliverance to the captives, and recovering of sight to the blind, to set at liberty them that are bruised." What about the rich? Was He sent to the rich? Let us see what He said about the rich.

> And he lifted up his eyes on his disciples, and said, blessed be ye poor: for yours is the kingdom of God … But woe unto you that are rich! For ye have received your consolation … Woe unto you, when all men shall speak well of you! For so did their fathers to the false prophets. (Luke 6:20, 24, and 26)

Let's look at this parable that Jesus gave about a man the Father blessed with plenty, and he kept it all for himself and did not give to the poor.

> And he spake a parable unto them, saying, the ground of a certain rich man brought forth plentifully: And he thought within himself, saying, what shall I do, because I have no room where to bestow my fruits? And he said, this will I do: I will pull down my barns, and build greater; and there will I bestow all my fruits and my goods. And I will say to my soul, Soul, thou hast much goods laid up for many years; take thine ease, eat, drink, and be merry. But God said unto him, Thou fool, this night thy soul shall be required of thee: then whose shall those things be,

> which thou hast provided? So is he that layeth up treasure for himself, and is not rich toward God. (Luke 12:16–21)

Here is what Mary, the mother of Jesus, said about the rich in Luke 1:53: "He hath filled the hungry with good things; and the rich he hath sent empty away." We read about a rich man named Zacchaeus. Jesus went to his house and spoke to him. We do not know what Jesus said to him, but he was convinced that he should get rid of his riches. Let us read what Zacchaeus said to Jesus.

> And, behold, there was a man named Zacchaeus, which was the chief among the publicans, and he was rich. And he sought to see Jesus who he was; and could not for the press, because he was little of stature. And he ran before, and climbed up into a sycomore tree to see him: for he was to pass that way. And when Jesus came to the place, he looked up, and saw him, and said unto him, Zacchaeus, make haste, and come down; for today I must abide at thy house. And he made haste, and came down, and received him joyfully. And when they saw it, they all murmured, saying, that he was gone to be guest with a man that is a sinner. And Zacchaeus stood, and said unto the Lord: Behold, Lord, the half of my goods I give to the poor; and if I have taken anything from any man by false accusation, I restore him fourfold. And Jesus said unto him, this day is salvation come to this

> house, forsomuch as he also is a son of Abraham. (Luke 19:2–9)

Here is what James the brother of Jesus wrote about rich men in James 5:1–3:

> Go to now, ye rich men, weep and howl for your miseries that shall come upon you. Your riches are corrupted, and your garments are motheaten. Your gold and silver is cankered; and the rust of them shall be a witness against you, and shall eat your flesh as it were fire. Ye have heaped treasure together for the last days.

In conclusion, I pray that you would be aware of the three main tools of Satan: (1) riches, (2) authority, and (3) promiscuity. With these he is trying to deceive the whole world so it will follow him. Look at your life. Make sure you are only having sex with one living husband or wife, be sure not to have any name above brethren in the body of Christ, and take care of the poor. I leave you with this Scripture spoken by Jesus.

> But when thou makest a feast, call the poor, the maimed, the lame, the blind: and thou shalt be blessed; for they cannot recompense thee: for thou shalt be recompensed at the resurrection of the just. (Luke 14:13–14)

God bless you.

(8)

Marriage and Divorce

In this sermon, marriage is the union of a man and a woman with the observance of a vow unto God, the heavenly Father that the union will remain until the separation by death. Let us read this excellent reminder from Jesus in Matthew 19:4–6:

> And he answered and said unto them, Have ye not read, that he which made them at the beginning made them male and female, And said, For this cause shall a man leave father and mother, and shall cleave to his wife: and they twain shall be one flesh? Wherefore they are no more twain, but one flesh. What therefore God hath joined together, let not man put asunder.

Should all Christians abide in the Word of God, there will be no room for divorce. Let's refresh our memories of this command the Father God has given unto women in Genesis 3:16: "Unto the woman he said, I will greatly multiply thy sorrow and thy conception; in sorrow thou shalt bring forth children; and thy desire shall be to thy husband, and he shall rule over thee." It is often said that this Scripture is not for today. To find out whether it is for today's life, let us pay attention to three points in that verse: (1) The Lord said that in sorrow the woman will bring forth children, which still exist today. (2) Her desire shall be for her husband. If her desire remains for her husband, there will be no room to desire another. (3) "And he shall rule over thee"—this is a saying most worldly women have a problem with. This is where you decide to obey God or be of the world; the choice is yours. If you are thinking about getting married or divorced, you want to understand this. No Christian should get a divorce. Jesus said that Moses, because of the hardness of the hearts of men, allowed men to put away their wives, Let us read Moses' law of divorce to the Jews.

> When a man hath taken a wife, and married her, and it come to pass that she find no favour in his eyes, because he hath found some uncleanness in her: then let him write her a bill of divorcement, and give it in her hand, and send her out of his house. And when she is departed out of his house, she may go and be another man's wife. (Deuteronomy 24:1–2)

Should the husband or wife of a Christian get a divorce, then the Christian should not remarry. Here is what Apostle Paul said in 1 Corinthians 7:10–11.

> And unto the married I command, yet not I, but the Lord, Let not the wife depart from her husband: But and if she depart, let her remain unmarried or be reconciled to her husband: and let not the husband put away his wife.

A Christian should not be of the world, as we understand in the words of Jesus in John 15:17–19:

> These things I command you, that ye love one another. If the world hate you, ye know that it hated me before it hated you. If ye were of the world, the world would love his own: but because ye are not of the world, but I have chosen you out of the world, therefore the world hateth you.

Do not follow the world with regard to divorce and remarriage. One of the signs of Jesus' return is that people will be marrying and divorcing for any cause. Hear the words of Jesus.

> But as the days of Noah were, so shall also the coming of the Son of man be. For as in the days that were before the flood they were eating and drinking, marrying and giving in marriage, until the day that Noe entered into the ark, And knew not until the flood came, and took them all away; so shall also the coming of the Son of man be. (Matthew 24:37–39)

The world uses Matthew 19:9 as grounds to divorce and remarry. Here is what Jesus said in Matthew 19:9: "And I say unto you, whosoever shall put away his wife, except it be for fornication, and shall marry another, committeth adultery: and whoso marrieth her which is put away doth commit adultery" (emphasis added). Let us now look at the word fornication and what Jesus meant by it. Fornication in the Bible is sexual intercourse between a man and a woman who are not married. The act of fornication, in the days of Jesus was committed by an espoused, betrothed, or engaged person, referred to as husband and wife, as seen in Matthew 1:18–20.

> Now the birth of Jesus Christ was on this wise: When as his mother Mary was espoused to Joseph, before they came together, she was found with child of the Holy Ghost. Then Joseph her husband, being a just man, and not willing to make her a public example, was minded to put her away privily. But while he thought on these things, behold, the angel of the LORD appeared unto him in a dream, saying, Joseph, thou son of David, fear not to take unto thee Mary thy wife: for that which is conceived in her is of the Holy Ghost. (Emphasis added)

Even though Mary and Joseph, the parents of Jesus, were not yet married, they were referred to as husband and wife. This is the wife Jesus referred to in Matthew 19:9 as committing fornication. To understand it better, no other woman after the mother of Jesus will be impregnated by the Power of the Most High. (There is no other Jesus to come.) Therefore should an espoused or engaged woman (wife) be found to be pregnant not by her fiancé (spouse), that has to be a result of fornication. Jesus said to put her away and in that case marry another. Let us take a look at the English construction of Matthew 19:9. We see the words "except it be for fornication" are between commas, which mean a different thought. Now let us use parentheses instead of commas. Matthew 19:9 says, "And I say unto you, whosoever shall put away his wife (except it be for fornication) and shall marry another, committeth adultery: and whoso marrieth her which is put away doth commit adultery." It will be good to note here that the New King James Version of the Holy Bible has the word fornication replaced by the words sexual immorality, which means fornication as well as adultery, which gives the world its right to divorce and remarry. However, Jesus cleared up the matter in Mark 10:9–12.

> What therefore God hath joined together, let not man put asunder. And in the house his disciples asked him again of the same matter. And he saith unto them, whosoever shall put away his wife, and marry another, committeth adultery against her. And if a woman shall put away her husband, and be married to another, she committeth adultery.

Notice that Jesus left out the part about fornication. Maybe it was too difficult for His disciples to understand how a wife could committed fornication or He did not want to refer to His parents.

Remember Malachi tells us that the Lord God hates divorce in Malachi 2:16: "For the LORD, the God of Israel, saith that he hateth putting away: for one covereth violence with his garment, saith the LORD of hosts: therefore take heed to your spirit that ye deal not treacherously."

There are some Christians who are already divorced; don't remarry. And there are some Christians who are already remarried, and there may be children in the marriage. How can I find a good word to say? That condition is left up to you. You can give up the marriage and serve God or stay in it and reject God. I believe that all children hate divorce, but you will have to explain to the child what is best for you. I say to you that the bed of that second marriage is defiled as long as the first spouse lives. Let me make it quite clear here: anyone who put away a spouse is to remain celibate according to the words Jesus in Mark 10:11–12 above.

A baker's dozen is thirteen; I leave with you a baker's dozen of things never to do in a marriage:

1. Never be too big to apologize.
2. Never go to sleep upset with each other.
3. Never stop communicating.
4. Never let a little dispute dissolve a great marriage.
5. Never compare your spouse to someone else.
6. Never allow a third party into your marriage.
7. Never fail to give your spouse a smile.
8. Never fail to compliment your spouse.
9. Never forget to spend some time together (just you two).
10. Never talk about your spouse's shortcomings with anyone.

11. Never punish your spouse by withholding sex.
12. Never dwell on a mistake made by your spouse.
13. Never call your spouse unlikeable names.

These things taken together will make a good marriage.

(9)

Is It Really Love When We Say, "I Love You"?

When Jesus (the only begotten Son of God our heavenly Father) was on this earth, His main topic was love. We say that we love Jesus, but we do not keep His commandments. Here Jesus said, "But I say unto you, Love your enemies, bless them that curse you, do good to them that hate you, and pray for them which despitefully use you, and persecute you." The Bible (King James Version) has some heartwarming quotes of love. Let us read some of them.

> For God so loved the world that he gave his only begotten Son, that whosoever believeth in him should not perish, but have everlasting life. For God sent not his Son into the world to condemn the world; but that the world through him might be saved. (John 3:16–17)

> He saith unto him the third time, Simon, son of Jonas, lovest thou me? Peter was grieved because

> he said unto him the third time, Lovest thou me? And he said unto him, Lord, thou knowest all things; thou knowest that I love thee. Jesus saith unto him, Feed my sheep. (John 21:17)

The apostle Paul whom Jesus sent to the Gentiles (that's you, if you are not a Jew) also taught love. First Corinthians 13:13 says, "And now abideth faith, hope, charity, these three; but the greatest of these is charity [impartial love]." Let us look at the three kinds of love.

1. Agape, God's love: John 14:23 says, "Jesus answered and said unto him, If a man love me, he will keep my words: and my Father will love him, and we will come unto him, and make our abode with him."

2. Eros, physical love: This is for husband and wife only. Genesis 4:1 says, "And Adam knew Eve his wife; and she conceived, and bare Cain, and said, I have gotten a man from the LORD." Genesis 24:67 says, "And Isaac brought her into his mother Sarah's tent, and took Rebekah, and she became his wife; and he loved her: and Isaac was comforted after his mother's death." Ephesians 5:28 says, "So ought men to love their wives as their own bodies. He that loveth his wife loveth himself."

> 3. Phileo, neighborly love: Matthew 22:39 says, "Jesus said, and the second is like unto it, Thou shalt love thy neighbour as thyself."

We as children of God should love like God, unconditionally, regardless of one's downfall. Here is how Paul put it:

> Be ye therefore followers of God, as dear children; and walk in love, as Christ also hath loved us, and hath given himself for us an offering and a sacrifice to God for a sweet-smelling savour … For ye were sometimes darkness, but now are ye light in the Lord: walk as children of light. (Ephesians 5:1–2 and 8)

For a better understanding of this message, fornication is committed by single persons, and adultery is committed by married or divorced persons. We say that we love God, yet we commit fornication and adultery. In most cases no one knows except for God, and He is the one we hurt most. The people on earth we love most—our daddy, mother, husband, or wife—do not want us to commit fornication and adultery, but when we do, most often they don't know. But God knows, and it hurts God, as we understand from this next Scripture:

> And God saw that the wickedness of man was great in the earth, and that every imagination of the thoughts of his heart was only evil continually.

> And it repented the LORD that he had made man on the earth and it grieved him at his heart. (Genesis 6:5–6)

Sex out of marriage now seems to be the norm, but it is still wrong. We say we love the Lord, but we don't abide in His commandments. These commandments were for the Jews only, but Jesus extended some laws to apply to the Gentiles. Exodus 20:14 says, "Thou shalt not commit adultery." Jesus said in Matthew 5:28, "But I say unto you, that whosoever looketh on a woman to lust after her hath committed adultery with her already in his heart." Jesus fulfilled the Law and confirmed the gospel. Luke 16:16 says, "The law and the prophets were until John: since that time the kingdom of God is preached, and every man presseth into it." Let us take a look at the Ten Commandments of God in part. (See Exodus 20:1–17 for the full commands.)

1. Thou shalt have no other gods before me.
2. Thou shalt not make unto thee any graven image.
3. Thou shalt not take the name of the Lord thy God in vain.
4. Remember the Sabbath day to keep it holy.
5. Honor thy father and thy mother.
6. Thou shalt not kill.
7. Thou shalt not commit adultery.
8. Thou shalt not steal.
9. Thou shalt not bear false witness against thy neighbor.
10. Thou shalt not covet [desire, want grudgingly] anything that is thy neighbor's.

Jesus simplified the Ten Commandments to two in Matthew 22:36–40: (1) love the Lord thy God with all thy heart [covers the first five], and (2) love thy neighbor as thyself [covers the last five]. Jesus said that upon these two are hang all the Law and the prophets.

If we really love the Lord, we will abide in (do) His words. Love is more action than words; Jesus said in John 14:15, "If ye love me keep my commandments" (emphasis added). In Ephesians 5:22, Paul said, "Wives, submit yourselves unto your own husbands, as unto the Lord" (emphasis added). In Ephesians 5:25 Paul said, "Husbands, love your wives, even as Christ also loved the church [not a building] and gave himself for it" (emphasis added). The Father will draw unto Jesus all who love Him and believe that Jesus is His Son.

Because I love you, I am saying these things to you so you might be saved from damnation. There are many people who are saved from death, as Jesus said to Martha in John 11:26: "And whosoever liveth and believeth in me shall never die. Believest thou this?" But if they are not saved from damnation, they will die when Jesus returns to paradise. Matthew 16:28 says, "Verily I say unto you, there be some standing here, which shall not taste of death, till they see the Son of man coming in his kingdom." We must ask the Father to draw us unto His Son, as Jesus said in John 6:44: "No man can come to me, except the Father which hath sent me draw him: and I will raise him up at the last day."

I am saying this to you because I love you; you must go to the Father in prayer and ask the Father to draw you unto His Son so you may be second saved or saved from damnation. There are many of our loved ones who have gone on before us. They believed but were not drawn to Jesus; they are in paradise-third heaven awaiting Jesus' return, and that is when they will die. We must live right so the Father will draw us unto His Son before we leave this earth. Otherwise we will die. There are many people I have tried to explain this to, but they would not let me. Some listened but they did not believe. You must understand and obey the gospel before your night comes; it will be far too late when you leave this earth.

It is hard sometimes to love our enemies, but that is a cross we must bear. We must love everyone in spite of not being loved, and we should not love anyone more than we love Jesus.

> Jesus said, He that loveth father or mother more than me is not worthy of me: and he that loveth son or daughter more than me is not worthy of me. And he that taketh not his cross, and followeth after me, is not worthy of me. (Matthew 10:37–38)

We say that we love our family and friends, but we end our lives and leave all those who loved us lonely and brokenhearted. Is that really love? Anyone who commits suicide is bound to go to hell, a place of torment, and may not see his or her loved ones again. Let us hear what a rich man said while in hell.

> And in hell he lift up his eyes, being in torments, and seeth Abraham afar off and Lazarus in his bosom ... Then he said, I pray thee therefore, father, that thou wouldest send him to my father's house: For I have five brethren; that he may testify

> unto them, lest they also come into this place of torment. (Luke 16:23, 27–28)

You do not want to go to hell. Jesus said we shouldn't worry about this life. Matthew 6:25 says, "Therefore I say unto you, Take no thought for your life, what ye shall eat, or what ye shall drink; nor yet for your body, what ye shall put on. Is not the life more than meat, and the body than raiment?" Luke 12:4–5 says, "And I say unto you my friends, be not afraid of them that kill the body, and after that have no more that they can do. But I will forewarn you whom ye shall fear: Fear him, which after he hath killed hath power to cast into hell; yea, I say unto you, Fear him."

Friend, there are many people who love you. Try telling your loved ones that you love them and see the love you will receive in return. Remember, if you take your life, it means you don't love God. Satan, who is a thief, stole Adam and Eve from God. He is a murderer and caused Cain to kill Abel. He tells you to take your life. Jesus said that He came to save life, not destroy it. Do you believe the Devil or Jesus? Remember, if you take your life, you will live again and answer to God for taking your life; therefore you will die a second death. I pray that you will truly love the Lord and do His will. Matthew 5:16 says, "Let your light so shine before men, that they may see your good works, and glorify your Father which is in heaven. Then the father will draw you unto His Son." John 6:65 says, "And he said, therefore said I unto you, that no man can come unto me, except it were given unto him of my Father." When the Father converts you and draws you to His Son, you will never die in this life or in the life to come. Jesus said He will give you eternal life.

> My sheep hear my voice, and I know them, and they follow me: And I give unto them eternal life; and they shall never perish, neither shall any man pluck them out of my hand. My Father, which gave them me, is greater than all; and no man is able to pluck them out of my Father's hand. (John 10:27–29)

Love means love. Look beyond the faults of others and love them anyway. Remember the wrong we all have done unto our Father God, and in spite of that, He loves us. In all things give God thanks.

God love and bless you.

(10)

Works of the Holy Spirit

First we want to understand that the Holy Ghost and the Holy Spirit even the Spirit of truth are one, and they are called the Comforter.

> If ye love me, keep my commandments. And I will pray the Father, and he shall give you another Comforter, that he may abide with you forever; Even the Spirit of truth; whom the world cannot receive, because it seeth him not, neither knoweth him: but ye know him; for he dwelleth with you, and shall be in you. [Understand that when you believe that Jesus is the Son of God, the Holy Spirit will dwell with you and when the Father converts you, the Holy Spirit dwells in you.] … But the Comforter, which is the Holy Ghost, whom the Father will send in my name, he shall teach you all things, and bring all things to your

> remembrance, whatsoever I have said unto you. (John 14:15–17, 26, emphasis added)

We also want to understand that the works of the Holy Ghost are physical and visual. Luke 3:22 says, "And the Holy Ghost descended in a bodily shape like a dove upon him, and a voice came from heaven, which said, Thou art my beloved Son; in thee I am well pleased." We also need to know that the Holy Spirit is mental and comforting. Revelation 2:7 says, "He that hath an ear, let him hear what the Spirit saith unto the churches; To him that overcometh will I give to eat of the tree of life, which is in the midst of the paradise of God." However, even though the Holy Spirit and the Holy Ghost work differently, they are all one and of God. John 4:24 says, "God is a Spirit: and they that worship him must worship him in spirit and in truth." Luke 4:1 says, "And Jesus being full of the Holy Ghost returned from Jordan, and was led by the Spirit into the wilderness."

Here is my testimony of the Holy Spirit in action. Concerning the baptism of water, I was converted for thirty-five years, at which time my grandson, who was seventeen years old, came to me and told me that the Holy Spirit had revealed to him that the birth of water Jesus spoke about in John 3:5 is not water baptism. I had a hard time seeing it that way until I sat with him and the boy I had taught all his life became my teacher. I remember the words of the Lord Jesus in Matthew 18:3–5: "You must be converted and become as a little child and humble yourself." After I saw what he was saying, I had a hard time believing that the meaning of the Scripture that I was taught (to be baptized by water) was wrong, but he was right. When I looked more closely at the Scripture and the Spirit gave me the true understanding, I had to go to my grandson and let him know that the blessings of Lord were upon him. I gave God thanks for him. Let us now look at the Scriptures and see what Jesus meant. To understand it clearly, we have to read John 3:3–6.

> Jesus answered and said unto him, Verily, verily, I say unto thee, Except a man be born again, he cannot see the kingdom of God. [Understand here Jesus meant born of the Spirit.] Nicodemus saith unto him, How can a man be born when he is old? Can he enter the second time into his mother's womb, and be born? Jesus answered, Verily, verily, I say unto thee, except a man be born of water and of the Spirit, he cannot enter into the kingdom of God. [The Spirit gave us the understanding that the water mentioned here is the water in the mother's womb.] That which is born of the flesh is flesh; and that which is born of the Spirit is spirit.

I give thanks to the heavenly Father for allowing His Holy Spirit to express to me the understanding of His holy word spoken by Christ Jesus, His only begotten Son, whom He brought to this earth assisted by His Holy Ghost. An angel confirmed this to Mary, the mother of Jesus, in Luke 1:35: "And the angel answered and said unto her, The Holy Ghost shall come upon thee, and the power of the Highest shall overshadow thee: therefore also that holy thing which shall be born of thee shall be called the Son of God."

Thank you to you for your understanding, and I pray that if He has not already, the Father will use you to teach these words unto others. Matthew 9:37–38 says, "Then saith he unto his disciples, The harvest truly is plenteous, but the labourers are few; Pray ye therefore the Lord of the harvest, that he will send forth labourers into his harvest. Amen."

God bless you.

(11)

A Look at the Family

This picture or view of the family is my understanding as related to the Holy Bible (KJV). It is under no circumstances my intention to oppress or lower anyone's standard. However, God loves you and wants you to live in accordance with His Word. As long as you are alive, you have the opportunity to do God's will. We do not want to wait until we cannot think and do for ourselves. Let us serve the Lord now. Here is what Jesus said while here on earth in John 9:4: "I must work the works of him that sent me, while it is day: the night cometh, when no man can work." Jesus' night came, and the Father is pleased with His work; will He be pleased with ours?

In the first family, God put Adam and Eve together [in marriage] and blessed them, and they became one flesh. Let us look at these Scriptures:

> And God blessed them, and God said unto them, be fruitful, and multiply, and replenish the earth, and subdue it: and have dominion over the fish

> of the sea, and over the fowl of the air, and over every living thing that moveth upon the earth. (Genesis 1:28)
>
> And Adam said, This is now bone of my bones, and flesh of my flesh: she shall be called Woman, because she was taken out of Man. Therefore shall a man leave his father and his mother, and shall cleave unto his wife: and they shall be one flesh. (Genesis 2:23–24)
>
> And Adam knew Eve his wife; and she conceived, and bare Cain, and said, I have gotten a man from the LORD. (Genesis 4:1)
>
> That is the first family.

No family is made unless God makes it. Unless God puts a man and a woman together, they are not lawfully together. When God puts a husband and wife together, they become one. When God blesses that man (I say man, which also means the woman because they are one) with a child, they become a family. Let me tell you about some misconceptions of the family. A man and woman who are not married who have a child or children are not a family. A man or woman with two or more living wives or husbands and children are not a family. A single woman with children is not a family. Single men with children are not a family. Two women with children are not a family. Two men with children are not a family. A widower or widow with children is a broken family. A divorced husband or wife with children is a broken family. (These people should not remarry unless their original wife or husband dies.) All sex out of marriage is wrong. It does not matter how much it is accepted by this world—it is still wrong in God's sight. Here are two sayings, one by David, who was king of Israel, and the next by his son Solomon, who was also the king of Israel. David said, "Except the Lord build the house, they labour in vain that build it: except the Lord keep the city, the watchman waketh but in vain." Psalm 127:1. Don't let Satan deceive you; only God can make a family. Solomon said, "There is a way that seemeth right unto a man, but the end thereof are the ways of death." Proverbs 16:25. The Father God wants to make and bless families; let us do what is right and, give God the opportunity.

As I conclude this message, the point I want to make is that if the family is not made by God, then it is of the world. The world sees it as a family, but God does not see it as a family. The Lord put us in the world, but He does not want us to be of the world. We are either of the world or of God. Jesus came all the way from heaven to earth to tell us not to have sex out of marriage and not to marry anyone who is divorced. Let us heed His words. God bless you.

(12)

What Is Your Relationship with God?

God sent His only begotten Son, Jesus the Christ, to redeem all people from their sins. First He went to the Jews, but they did not receive Him or believe that He is God's Son. Jesus returned to the Father brokenhearted and disappointed. Before He returned, He made a third category of people, which are called Christians. Both Jews and Gentiles have to be converted to Christianity (Matthew 18:3).

Gentiles were and some still are condemned, outcast, ostracized, abandoned, lost, deserted, and left alone by God. To put it simply, God had turned His back on the Gentiles and now even the Jews; they allowed Satan to take control of their lives. All people who believe that Jesus is the Son of God are forgiven of their sins (John 3:16), and all who do the will of God are converted or born again. Here is what Jesus said to the Pharisees (leaders of the Jews) in John 8:44: "Ye are of your father the devil, and the lusts of your father ye will do. He was a murderer from the beginning, and abode not in the truth, because there is no truth in him. When he speaketh a lie, he speaketh of his own: for he is a liar, and the father of it."

Because Adam disobeyed God and sinned, God has forever placed that sin upon everyone who comes into this world. God said that we would die, and Satan said we would not surely die; here is what God said to Adam and Eve. Genesis 2:17 says, "But of the tree of the knowledge of good and evil, thou shalt not eat of it: for in the day that thou eatest thereof thou shalt surely die." Now hear what Satan said to Eve in Genesis 3:4: "And the serpent said unto the woman, ye shall not surely die." The apostle Paul said because Adam sinned, all of us sin. Romans 5:12 says, "Wherefore, as by one man sin entered into the world and death by sin; and so death passed upon all men, for that all have sinned." However, God sent His Son into the world to take away that sin.

It is worthy to be noted here that before Jesus came to earth in the flesh, no Gentiles were forgiven of their sins; they all died without salvation until the Savior came. Jesus came into the world and gave salvation to all who believe, and He wants us to ask the Father to draw us unto Him so He can take us to the Father. Here is what Jesus went to do for us:

> In my Father's house are many mansions: if it were not so, I would have told you. I go to prepare a place for you. And if I go and prepare a place for you, I will come again, and receive you unto myself; that where I am, there ye may be also. (John 14:2–3)

What is your relationship with God? Be you a Jew or Gentile, you must first believe that Jesus is the Messiah and Son of God. You must second do well to all mankind and third pray that the

Lord will draw you unto His Son. Remember, God is Spirit and those who worship Him must worship Him in Spirit and in truth. Keep these things in mind when you go to God in prayer.

> And when thou prayest, thou shalt not be as the hypocrites are: for they love to pray standing in the synagogues and in the corners of the streets, that they may be seen of men. Verily I say unto you, they have their reward. But thou, when thou prayest, enter into thy closet, and when thou hast shut thy door, pray to thy Father which is in secret; and thy Father which seeth in secret shall reward thee openly. But when ye pray, use not vain repetitions, as the heathen do: for they think that they shall be heard for their much speaking. Be not ye therefore like unto them: for your Father knoweth what things ye have need of, before ye ask him. (Matthew 6:5–8)

I pray that you, if you don't already, will have a good relationship with the Father, and I also pray that He will continue to use us in His harvest.

God bless you.

(13)

Jesus' Twelve Disciples

I used the books of Mark and Acts to point out the names of Jesus' twelve disciples (King James Version).

> And he ordained twelve, that they should be with him, and that he might send them forth to preach, And to have power to heal sicknesses, and to cast out devils: And Simon he surnamed Peter; And James the son of Zebedee, and John the brother of James; and he surnamed them Boanerges, which is, The sons of thunder: And Andrew, and Philip, and Bartholomew, and Matthew, and Thomas, and James the son of Alphaeus, and Thaddaeus, and Simon the Canaanite, And Judas Iscariot, which also betrayed him: and they went into a house. (Mark 3:14–19)

> So they proposed two men: Joseph called Barsabbas (also known as Justus) and Matthias. Then they

> prayed, "Lord, you know everyone's heart. Show us which of these two you have chosen to take over this apostolic ministry, which Judas left to go where he belongs." Then they cast lots, and the lot fell to Matthias; so he was added to the eleven apostles. (Acts 1:23–26)

1. Simon Bar-Jonas/Jesus surnamed Peter
2. James the son of Zebedee/Jesus surnamed them Boanerges, which means sons of thunder
3. John the brother of James/Boanerges, which means sons of thunder
4. Andrew son of Jonas/brother of Simon Peter
5. Philip
6. Bartholomew
7. Matthew the tax collector
8. Thomas the doubter
9. James the son of Alphaeus
10. Thaddaeus, also known as Judas, son of James
11. Simon the Canaanite, the Zealot
12. Judas Iscariot, who also betrayed Jesus and killed himself
13. Matthias, chosen to take over the apostolic ministry Judas Iscariot left. Some Bible teachers view Matthias as an invalid apostle and believe that Paul was God's choice to replace Judas Iscariot as the twelfth apostle.

God's grace is with us.

(14)

Highlight These Scriptures In Your Holy Bible (King James Version) Be Sure To Read Them:

Here is the true understanding of the word of God. I want you to first read and highlight what the Prophet Isaiah said about the Jews and by extension the Gentiles long before Jesus came to earth; Jesus said it to the Jews when he was upon the earth; and now by His Holy Word, He is saying it to us: that we are teaching for doctrine the commandments of men. Isaiah 29:13 / Matthew 15:8-9. Here are three commandments of men:

1. Call a building church; how confusing; is the church a building or a body of believers converted by the Father and drawn unto His Son? Matthew 16:18. Jesus begun building the church on the day of Pentecost; Peter preached the first sermon and three thousand souls were added to the church, not a building. Satan is using the building called church to try and prevail against the true church (Jesus' sheep) John 10:27:

2. Come into the building to worship the Father; Jesus said that it just cannot happen, John 4:21-24 Matthew 6:5. He said go and teach Matthew 28:19; neither Jesus, nor His disciples including Paul built a building and called it church. There is so much work to do in the field, why would anyone want to waste time in the building. More over the Father sent Jesus to invite the Gentiles to His heavenly home. The Father said bring them from the highways and hedges, Luke 14:23, that is where Jesus wants us to go; tell the poor that they must live right Matthew 5:16. And
3. Altar call; why are the Hirelings (Jeremiah 3:15, Jer.23:1-2, John 10:11-15) calling people to come to an altar, and telling them to give Jesus their heart, He will save them? That cannot happen as you would see in the scriptures below. Jesus said once you believe that He is the Christ, you are saved even before you entered the building unlawfully called church. Jesus said that you must go/pray to the Father in His name and ask the Father to draw you unto Him, John 14:6 [this means two things; only in Jesus' name can you pray to the Father and only Jesus can take you to the Father] John 6:65. Jesus prayed to the Father that He would draw Peter unto Him Luke 22:32. The Father is seeking from the heart who He wants to worship Him. Therefore altar call and the buildings are null and void. We must understand that God's chosen people the Jews only had two buildings built unto God and He destroyed them both, 1Kings 9:1-9 and Mark 13 :1-2, because of the hardness of their hearts. Here is

> where God forsook the Jews (Jeremiah 23:39, Amos 7:8, Amos 8:2, Luke 14:24, Acts 13:46, and Lamentations 2:6-9) [verse 8 tells of the veiling wall, a reminder from Solomon's temple, exist even to this day]. David King of the Jews, a man after God's own heart, was not worthy enough to build a building unto God, how can a Gentile build any? Last point, no house unto the Lord will ever be built out of the Holy City in Jerusalem.

Let us remember that we must worship in Spirit and in truth. All the Lord requires from us is a pure heart John 4:23. We are to do good works unto our fellowmen Matthew 5:16 and we shall be rewarded not on earth but in heaven Matthew 6:1 and Matthew 16:27.

Be sure to highlight these scriptures in your KJV bible in order to find them quickly when you are teaching others about the word of God.

Three Gods in one: 1John 5:7. Three heavens: First Genesis 1:1, Second Genesis 1:16-17, and Third Genesis 1:6-8 and 20 [Paradise where the birds fly]. Luke 23:43, 2Corinthians 12:2-4. [Not the Paradise in first heaven, Revelation 2:7].

Salvation is from the Father God himself He sent His Son Jesus with it first to the Jews; John 4:22, after which to the Gentiles Luke 14:23.

Two saves:

The first is saved from death; John 1:11-12, John 3:16-18, John 11:25-26, Mark16:16, and Acts 13:39. However let us consider what Jesus said in Matthew 16:28, Matthew 7:21-23, and Matthew 8:11-12.

Second save is saved from damnation; Only the Father can second save us, draw us unto His Son; John 6:44-45, Luke 22:31-32, John 10:27-29, and Matthew 25:31-34.

Abraham's Bosom: Believers/Saints and Sheep in hell. Luke 16:22-23, though they be dead yet shall they live, John 11:25, other sheep not of this fold John 10:16, Jesus brought them out of Hell Matthew 27:52, and Hell has enlarged Herself, Isaiah 5:14. Therefore Jesus has made the Third Heaven/Paradise the only Fold where the Believers, Sheep, Saints will tarry until Jesus return, John 21:22. Pray that the Father will draw you unto His Son Jesus, if not already. I pray that the Father will use you in His harvest, Luke 10:2. Come out of the building called church, wasting time that you could be working for the Lord, there is much work out there to do, time is short and there are not many workers. Make sure Jesus does not turn you away, Matthew 8:11-12. Thanks. God bless you.

(15)

How-to Pray

First we must know and understand that the heavenly Father is Spirit, John 4:23 and we must allow our Spirit to be in communion with Him; this can only be done by using Jesus' name John 14:6. The best way for our Spirit to contact the Father's Spirit is to be alone in a quiet place, Matthew 6:5-8 and not be loud. We must not repeat or be repetitious in our request to God, because the Father knows our heart's desire even before we ask of Him.

Secondly we must understand that our talking to the Father is a conversation and in any conversation we must allow the other person time to speak; therefore when we say what we want to say unto the Lord, we should at some time be still and quiet, listen to what the Father through His Holy Spirit John 14:26 will say unto us. Meditate on what we said unto the Lord and hear His reply. If there be no reply, that do not means He did not hear us; however we are to have faith that what we had asked for, we shall receive it. Understand that the Lord will meet our needs not our greed.

Thirdly the Lord does not hear the prayer of Sinners John 9:31 that is anyone who do not believe that Jesus Christ is the begotten

Son of God. Once we believe that Jesus is God's Son then we have power to become sons of God John 1:11-12 and He will hear our prayers. If we do not believe that Jesus is the Messiah, Son of God John 3:18 then there is no need to pray because we can only pray in Jesus' name John 14:6.

Fourthly we must pray to the Father that He will convert us and draw us unto His Son Jesus Luke 22:32 and John 6:44. The Father has sent an invitation to us inviting us to His heavenly home Luke 14:23, therefore we must reply (R.S.V.P.) to the Father that He will make a space available for us at His supper table. Only Jesus can take us there John 14:6. We must show the Father that we really want to come by getting the right garments to attend; that is to hate no man and do well to all mankind. Remember that the Father is seeking from the heart Matthew 18:35 and Matthew 15:8-9 whom He wants to attend His supper Luke 14:24. We must always pray. from the heart; that means we must fulfill our promises that we made to God in prayer by doing God's will.

Fifthly we should honor and respect the God head by men praying with head uncovered and women praying with head covered. 2 Corinthians 11:3-8. Prayers to God are like music to us; it is understood in all languages. When Jesus was upon the earth, He gave an example of how we should pray to the Father Matthew 6:9-13. Whenever we have food to eat, we should not forget to Give God thanks for providing it and ask His blessings upon it that it would do our bodies good, not forgetting the hands that labored to bring it before us. Do not forget, It is a shame for a man to pray and to sit at a dinner table with his head covered.

A Testimony of prayer:

I will be remised in my goal not to tell of this testimony. I pray that it will be an encouragement to all of my unfortunate brothers and sisters whom Satan has struck with that dreadful and undesired sickness or discomfort condition called cancer (hate to use the word).

Once again the Lord God Almighty, (Genesis 6:3 and Exodus 3:15 this is where the father tells us what to call Him), Exhibited His goodness, mercy, and power to my wife and me.

This is a short version of the testimony, (Jesus tells us if we believe, we shall receive Matthew 21:22).

As I recalled in the first part of the year 2011, Satan has attempted to put cancer upon my wife when the family's Doctor informed my daughter, who is a Nurse, that her mother has cancer. She informed me by telephone and she sounded very distraught. I told her to cheer up and allow me to contact the great physician and not to tell her Mom. I went to the Lord in prayer and told Him that if my wife is ill then I am ill because He made us one. I also asked Him to please remove that cancer from my wife. My daughter told me that the results of the biopsy were expected in three days. I told her to have faith there is no cancer, and the results of the biopsy proved just that. I give Thanks unto the Lord; my wife is free from cancer up to this day.

Again at the ending part of the same year 2011, after having a routine checkup by the family's Doctor, he informed me that I had prostate cancer. I told him, that is not so. He said "let us see what the specialist has to say." I again went to the Lord in prayer and asked that He allowed me a few more minutes on earth to spread His word some more, and to see my last daughter graduate (she should be graduating in 2015). I gave God thanks and went my way with a positive attitude. However my family was not happy with my decision not to have the biopsy. One day the Holy Spirit asked me who all was in that situation with me. At that point I realized that I had to do the biopsy for my family sake. I went to an independent specialist recommended by my daughter (nurse). He did a next test and repeated to me the same words that my family's doctor said, "in all my years of practice I have not seen a PSA that high without being cancer." I got the biopsy done and the results came out negative. I gave thanks unto God once again for His mercies which endure forever.

Finally when we pray, we do not want to go into synagogues and corner of streets lifting up hands and using big words to be seen and heard of men. We are to anoint, rest hands on and pray for the sick and according to their and our faith, they shall be heal. I pray that the Lord's blessings abide and remain upon us always Amen.

(16)

My Favorite Testimony

In 1974 my wife and I had three children, two girls and one boy, all of whom were plagued with asthma. Their ages were four, two, and going on one. They had to be admitted to the hospital for treatment very often. When one would come out, another would go in, and sometimes two were in the hospital at the same time. It became very burdensome to go to nursery, school, work, and hospital visits, but we definitely did not want to lose any of our children.

One day while our baby girl was in the hospital, my wife and I had just retired to bed when we heard a radio announcement requesting that we come to the hospital urgently. We rushed to the hospital; there we met a team of doctors around the crib with an oxygen tent, and our baby girl was there gasping for air as if it was her last breath. The attending physician told us that she was not responding to any of the medication and there was nothing else they could do.

At that point I got down on my knees and prayed to the Father God and asked Him to please leave the child with us, but if it was His will that she go, then let His will be done. When I had finished praying and got up, most of the doctors were gone and the child was breathing normally. I gave God thanks for hearing my cry and leaving the precious child with us. The doctor said that he would discharge her the next day.

The next day when the doctor discharged her, he told us to try not to let her return because her body was unresponsive to the medication. On our way out of the hospital, when we got downstairs and were walking toward the exit, a nurse stopped us and said she always saw us in and out the hospital with the kids and she did not know where we live but we had water that was settled around the house to go and fill it in. I told her okay and thanks. We did not ask her name. I asked the wife if she knew her, and she said no. At that time the hospital in Nassau, Bahamas, was small, and my wife was good at remembering names and faces. I was also a policeman and fireman and was always in and out of the hospital, and I do not remember seeing that nurse before or after that occasion. I filled in the water puddle in front of our home, and none of the children ever had asthma again. Thanks to God and also that special nurse, as well as the hospital's doctors and staff. That baby girl has become a registered nurse. God bless you.

Acknowledgments

I give thanks to the almighty God and His only begotten Son with the inspiration of His Holy Spirit. Let us not forget Jesus' disciples and loved ones, who we read about. Much literature has been left behind by our fellow writers so we may understand and receive salvation.

To my dad, Jesse, and mom, Tessa, (who has gone on), and their lovely children, a wonderful family that the heavenly Father has sent me through. They really impacted my life and my early Christian education. Thanks to all.

I say thanks to my sweet wife, Nancy, and her family, as well as our six gifts from God and their spouses, Dawn and Emery, Dennie, Dion and Marcia, Donald II and Clara, Douro and Belinda, and our baby girl, Dien, along with our seven grand-jewels, all of whom brought comfort and joy to me while I was writing this book.

Thanks to other supporting members of my family, my hardworking brothers and sisters in the Lord, all of whom in some way aided in this book;

I must not forget the pleasant staff at Westbow Press that I communicated with from beginning to end; you all made my work so easy, I say thanks. May God continue to bless you all.

Synopses of the Author's early life, marriage life, career, Christian life, evangelism ministry, and how he got to publishing the book.

Born and grew up in Nassau Bahamas, my Dad was killed in a traffic accident, by a drunk driver; I was eleven at the time, the fifth of nine children. Our Mom did not want to separate us; therefore she took us out of school at fourteen years old (the mandatory school age at that time) to work for support of the family.

Brought up in a family that love and respect God, I had always prayed and asked the Lord to give me a wife that would lead me to Him. I was living in the East and a young girl name Nancy age seventeen just out of school, living in the West, came in the East to work. I met Nancy, she attended a small Church in eight Street the Grove Ministered by James Redman and Donald Dorsett, we got married there in 1972 and the Father has drawn me unto His Son in 1973 under that ministry. We are blessed with six children; all are alive, and happily together, thanks be to God.

The Lord has taken me through the Royal Bahamas Police Force, from 1969 to 1999, in which I had never wavered in the faith, I had stumbled, because I am human, however with the Lord's help, not to make the same mistakes again, I am much stronger. I say to my brothers in the Forces, Keep God in front.

Upon leaving the Police Force, Nancy and I moved to the USA where we now reside. I started to work for myself, only to understand that the Lord Jesus had His work planned out for me to do. He has been grooming me over the years and in 2006 the Holy Spirit instructed me to put out a DVD, LET ALL THE WORLD BELIEVE.

The Spirit later informed me that 95 per cent or more Bahamians believe and are saved according to John 1:11-12, John 3:16-17, and John 11:26-26. And that DVD is not for Believers. Therefore I was instructed to produce the second DVD, FINAL HOUR. To mention the production of the DVDs, I was seeking professional production, but the Holy Spirit said to me that if He wanted professional He would have gotten professionals. He also reminded me that the Jews rejected the Son of God because He was menial to them. Please do not be proud, listen to what the words are saying. I have also put out a number of sermons on paper. I believe they will go to whom they are intended. Only God knows.

I also put out a CD, OUR FATHER SONG #1, I don't know how I did it. It only could have been the guidance of the Holy Spirit to put the words and scriptures to rhyme like that. I am still amazed. All the understanding of God's word mentioned in the CD, I have received in the past four years. I am happy that I received it and that I am able to pass it on to you. I am also happy that the Holy Spirit had led me to Minister Outten who with his team did such a wonderful job. I was happy to start giving them out in 2014. You may be able to hear it (Our Father Song #1) on YouTube.

It was at the beginning of summer 2014 when I was on the internet and I saw this Christian website Westbow Press, encouraging Christians to write books. At that time I had two sermons prepared which I was waiting on the Holy Spirit to tell me where and when to deliver them. While on the website I understand the Holy Spirit saying to me publish the sermons in book. I must agree I was a little skeptic because I had never before published a book nor did I know how to. However, anyone who know about the Holy Spirit, when He gives you something to do and you don't do it right away, it can lay heavily upon you. The website was so well put together and convincing that I went for it and with God's help this is the end results. Thanks for reading.

God bless you.